Enabling Communication
in Children with Autism

Enabling Communication in Children with Autism

Carol Potter
and
Chris Whittaker

Jessica Kingsley Publishers
London and Philadelphia

The right of Carol Potter and Chris Whittaker to be identified as authors of this work has been asserted by them in accordance with the Copyright, Designs and Patents Act 1988.

First published in the United Kingdom in 2001 by
Jessica Kingsley Publishers Ltd,
116 Pentonville Road, London
N1 9JB, England

and

325 Chestnut Street,
Philadelphia PA 19106, USA.

www.jkp.com

© Copyright 2001 Carol Potter and Chris Whittaker

Library of Congress Cataloging in Publication Data

A CIP catalog record for this book is available from the Library of Congress

British Library Cataloguing in Publication Data

A CIP catalogue record for this book is available from the British Library

ISBN 1 85302 ??? ?

Printed and Bound in Great Britain by
Athenaeum Press, Gateshead, Tyne and Wear

Contents

List of Figures and Tables

Figures

Tables

This book is dedicated to our parents:
Stanley and Brenda Potter and
the late Chris and Mary Whittaker.

Acknowledgements

We would like to thank the Joseph Rowntree Foundation for funding our two-year research project and the Shirley Foundation for additional support during the writing up period.

Our warmest appreciation must go to all of those who took part in our study. Experience of the individual personality of each child, so easily lost in research summaries, was a very positive benefit that has remained with us. Classroom teams, speech and language therapists, as well as senior managers, were extremely welcoming and generous with their time throughout the research period. Many thanks also to parents for allowing their children to take part in the study. We should like to take this opportunity to wish them and their children well in the future.

Grateful thanks are due to the members of our Project Advisory Group for their expert advice: Dr Joan Adams, Betsy Brua, Professor David Galloway, Brenda Nally, Julie Richardson, David Sherratt and Rosemary Tozer, and also to Professor Carol Fitz-Gibbon. Sincere thanks to Dr Emma Stone of the Joseph Rowntree Foundation for her extremely supportive and perceptive assistance during the project. We also want to thank Janet Linehan and Dr Thomas Linehan for their continuing interest in our work and unfailing personal support.

Finally, we are happy to acknowledge that the views, interpretations and conclusions, along with any omissions or possible errors, are entirely our own responsibility.

Carol Potter and Chris Whittaker
4th August 2000

Foreword

About This Book

This book aims to help school-based staff develop more communication-enabling environments for children with autism who use little or no speech, although we sincerely hope that parents will also find many sections helpful. The book is based on a two-year research project that was undertaken in five special schools in the UK. A clear intention throughout the text is to establish a strong link between our own research, theoretical issues, and what goes on in real classrooms on a daily basis. To achieve this end, many practice scenarios are included to illustrate communication-enabling approaches in action.

In our research, we found that when practitioners adopted a range of communication-enabling strategies and approaches, which built on the children's strengths, those children with autism and minimal or no speech involved were able to make relatively significant progress in their social and communication abilities. This study also demonstrated that factors within the environment, rather than within the child, were influential in affecting the rate and quality of the children's spontaneous communication. These findings have implications for ways in which autism is researched and for professional training in this field.

This was a study where five classrooms and 18 children were observed in depth, but over a relatively short period of time. We strongly recommend, in Chapter 11, that more classrooms and children are examined in detail and over time. The focus should be, as in this study, on examining ways in which their environment can be more or less enabling.

How the Book is Organized

The first chapter gives an overview of autism and the changing approaches to intervention in the area of communication. The critical importance of spontaneous communication is discussed, together with an overview of the nature of communication environments. Chapter 2 describes our research project and summarizes key findings. Subsequent chapters provide in-depth discussion of the practical implications of these findings. In Chapter 3, we explore the impact of adult speech on the communication ability of children with autism and describe the use and effectiveness of a minimal speech approach. Chapter 4 examines the benefits of using Proximal Communication to foster interaction, while Chapter 5 discusses the advantages of a continuum approach to prompting in order to elicit communication that is more spontaneous. Ways of introducing children to effective communication systems are considered in Chapter 6; while Chapter 7 explains how high quality communication opportunities can be provided for children in everyday school activities. Chapter 8 discusses possible strategies for enabling children with autism to begin to communicate with each other, and Chapter 9 outlines classroom management approaches to help implement effective communication-enabling approaches. Chapter 10 explores the current curricular context in relation to the themes discussed in the book and finally Chapter 11 summarizes findings, outlines limitations and explores the implications of our work for professional training and for intervention studies.

The Need for Reflection

We must emphasize that what is presented in the following pages is not a simple step-by step guide where strict adherence to a formula will lead to a perfect result every time. We fully acknowledge the danger that by describing these approaches in an accessible way, they may appear simple and easy to implement. It should be recognized, however, that creating high quality communication-enabling environments for children with autism and minimal or no speech is a complex, demanding and time-consuming undertaking. It requires skill, knowledge, understanding, emotional resilience and, for some professionals, perhaps a radical shift in attitude. What we are outlining are principles and approaches that adults will need to develop into skilful practice, use flexibly and reflect upon – both while they are using them and subsequently.

What Sort of Framework?

The approaches described in this book draw on what is known about communication development in early childhood and how this knowledge can be used to enhance the communication of children similar to those in our study. These approaches emphasize structure, consistency, breaking down tasks into manageable steps and social support of children's communication behaviours. They are, however, employed within an ethos that stresses flexibility and responsiveness to the child's spontaneous communication, with a clear focus on the children's capacities.

We also place a strong emphasis on the role that the environment plays in enabling or disabling the children's progress. Professional practice, crucially including attitudes as well as knowledge and skills, is highlighted as having a major impact on both the amount and type of the children's communication. This focus on children's strengths and the important role of the environment is very different from the prevalent 'deficit model' of autism, in which the 'problem' is located within the child.

Successful Relationships:
A Context for Successful Teaching

Finally, it is important to state our fundamental belief that high quality interpersonal relationships between adults and children lie at the heart of all successful teaching. Although we would argue that the approaches discussed in this book could significantly enhance the development of such relationships with children with autism and minimal speech, we strongly believe that the relationships themselves are much more than the sum of any such approaches.

Introduction

Autism: Needs and Strengths

Literature in the field of autism has generally emphasized the nature of the impairments which individuals experience. Happé (1994) summarized the triad of impairments which characterize these difficulties as:

(a) qualitative impairment in reciprocal social interaction

(b) qualitative impairment in verbal and non-verbal communication and in imaginative activity

(c) a markedly restricted repertoire of activities and interests. (Happé 1994, p.20)

Clearly, such impairments exert very significant effects on the everyday life experiences of people with autism, with those individuals who do not develop speech being particularly disempowered.

While research identifying autism specific 'deficits' has greatly informed our understanding of what autism is, an exclusive emphasis on impairment alone may result in a range of inappropriate beliefs about the potential of these individuals, which in turn may adversely affect their prospects for a good quality of life. For example, Hurley-Geffner (1995) argued that continued exclusive emphasis on the communication and social difficulties of children with autism has led some practitioners to believe that such individuals are incapable of communicating effectively or engaging in meaningful relationships. As a consequence, few interventions have been devised to facilitate developmental areas such as friendship, for example (Potter 1996).

A closer inspection of the literature, however, reveals that, despite their significant difficulties, children with autism do possess certain communicative strengths within contexts that are enabling. For example, Whittaker (1996) highlighted the finding of Sigman *et al.* (1986) that children with autism engaged in *equal* amounts of joint eye gaze as typically developing children and children with severe learning disabilities, when engaged in social games which did not involve objects. McHale *et al.* (1980) reported that the social responsiveness of children with autism varied 'in a normal way' when interacting with familiar as opposed to unfamiliar adults. It was also found that some children with autism could engage in spontaneous symbolic play when taught to do so within a structured and enjoyable context (Sherratt 1999).

In this book, we will adopt a 'capacity' perspective on the communication abilities of children with autism and little or no speech by focusing on the progress that they can achieve when their everyday environments are communication enabling.

Perspectives on Communication Interventions

What sorts of approaches to communication intervention have been employed in recent years? In the 1950s and early 1960s, when a psychoanalytical approach to autism was current, language and communication were not considered targets for intervention, since difficulties in these areas were viewed as an expression of inner conflicts, which themselves had resulted in autism. With the wane of such theories, a behaviourist approach gained ground during the 1960s and 1970s, where children were rewarded for producing targeted communicative behaviours in clinical settings (for example, Lovaas 1977). As it became apparent that behaviours learnt in these settings were not being generalized to everyday environments, a much greater emphasis on functional communication emerged, that is communication which benefits children directly in their everyday living environments (for example, Goetz, Schuler and Sailor 1981). More recently, enabling people with autism to communicate spontaneously in everyday situations has been identified as a critical goal (Charlop and Haymes 1994; Potter and Whittaker 1997; Sigafoos and Littlewood 1999; Watson *et al.* 1989). Research has rarely focused on enabling children with autism and minimal speech to interact more spontaneously, hence the emphasis of our research.

Why is Spontaneity Important?

The entitlement of all children to 'freedom of expression' has been enshrined in Article 13 of the United Nations Convention on the Rights of the Child 1989, which stated that children must have 'freedom to seek, receive and impart information and ideas of all kinds' (Article 13).

This declaration is completely inclusive so that children with significant communication impairments are also fully entitled to these rights. One fundamental aspect of achieving this freedom of expression is the ability to communicate spontaneously: that is to be able to *initiate* interactions with others in order to convey one's needs and wants. The importance of this attribute cannot be overemphasized, since it is the means through which individuals begin to exert control over their own lives. Charlop and Trasowech (1991) stated that spontaneous communication is vital because it naturalizes children's communication, allows them to participate in social interactions and is a means by which they can make their needs and wants known.

Being able to initiate communication is so familiar to most people that it is often taken for granted. For people with communication impairments, however, there may be significant barriers to the achievement of this goal.

At present, there is little emphasis on spontaneity in current educational practice. A central theme of this book is that enabling children with autism to communicate spontaneously should constitute a major goal throughout their educational careers.

Concepts of Autism and Expectations

Current concepts of autism may, in part, be responsible for a lack of emphasis on teaching children with autism to initiate communication. There may be a belief that children with autism cannot communicate spontaneously because of their autism. Possibly as a consequence of this, a number of authors have noted that approaches which teach children how to *respond*, rather than how to *initiate* communication, are more likely to have been employed (Charlop and Haymes 1994; Halle 1987; Potter 1997).

It is a fundamental premise of this book that being able to respond and being able to communicate spontaneously are two different abilities and need to be taught using different approaches.

Spontaneous Communication and Children with Autism

The generally accepted view is that many children with autism experience significant difficulty in initiating communication (Carr and Kolinsky 1983; Charlop and Haymes 1994; Landry and Loveland 1988; Stone and Caro-Martinez 1990; Stone *et al.* 1997; Watson *et al.* 1989). Stone and Caro-Martinez (1990) found that, on average, children with autism communicated only three or four times per hour in unstructured school situations. By contrast, typically developing children have been found to communicate around two hundred times per hour (Wetherby *et al.* 1988).

Research on the spontaneous communication of children with autism has usually focused on the children themselves, with researchers recording only aspects of the children's communication, without referring to the possible influence of factors in their immediate communication environment (for example, Stone and Caro-Martinez 1990; Watson, Martin and Schaffer 1986).

Focus on Communication Environments

Our two-year research project sought to explore the issue of spontaneous communication from a different perspective. We wanted to move the focus away from exclusively concentrating on the children themselves to find out, instead, if aspects of their communication environment enabled or disabled them in their attempts to become spontaneous communicators. We use the term *communication environment* to refer to 'those aspects of the environment that influence the individual's ability to communicate' (Bradshaw 1998, p.62). In other words, we wanted to find out if some children with autism rarely initiate communication simply because they have autism, or because aspects of their communication environment are not sufficiently enabling.

Van der Gaag and Dormandy (1993) noted that the concept of a 'communication environment' is relatively recent. A number of procedures have been developed which assess aspects of the communication environment (Rowland and Schweigert 1993; van der Gaag 1988).

Key social and environmental factors thought to influence the abilities of those with significant communication impairments are summarized in Figure 1.1 (p.18).

To this extensive list, we would add that the nature of the *spoken* environment is particularly important for children such as those in our study: that is to say the amount and complexity of speech which adults use with these children in everyday settings (Potter and Whittaker 1999). The creation of varied high quality opportunities for communication within the context of enjoyable and meaningful activities should also constitute a central feature of the communication environment for children with autism and little or no speech. Further in-depth discussion of these issues is found in later chapters.

Our research was specifically undertaken in the children's own everyday communication environments, since children with autism have often demonstrated greater social abilities in naturalistic rather than experimental settings (Toomey and Adams 1995). Two contrasting classroom sessions observed during the project highlight the environmental focus of the research and are outlined in Box 1.1 (p.19). Both took place after we had completed our collection of data in this particular classroom, so we were able to suggest changes to practice which did not interfere with the balance of our data. Any of the other scenarios in this book, which involved us in giving advice on changes of practice, similarly took place after data collection had been completed.

Key Aspects of a Communication Environment
Bradshaw (1998)

- Physical properties of the environment (noise and light).
Peck (1989)
- The nature of opportunities for communication that children encounter in their everyday lives.
- General characteristics of the school or residential setting in which the children spend their time.
Rowland and Schweigert (1993)
- Characteristics of the activities in which children engage (e.g. enjoyable, chosen by the child, terminated by the child?).
- The adequacy of children's communication systems.
- Characteristics of adult styles of interaction (e.g. do they give children enough time to respond?).
- Communication-enabling qualities of materials (e.g. do they offer turn-taking opportunities?).
- Specific opportunities for communication.
van der Gaag and Dormandy (1993)
- Policy issues (do policy statements in individual establishments emphasize integration in the local community?).
- Structure (assessment of day-to-day running issues of establishments – for example, roles and responsibilities of staff).
- Resources available to clients.

Figure 1.1 Key aspects of a communication environment

Box 1.1

Enabling and Disabling Communication

Scenario 1

Simon is a young child with an attractive and mischievous person-ality who has autism. His teacher told us that he understood little spoken language and that he rarely initiated communication with anyone. During a snack session he sat at the table, without attempting to communicate what he wanted. The teacher went around the table and when it was Simon's turn, she said: 'Which one do you want Simon, orange or lemon?' and then she almost immediately physically prompted him to point to one of the containers.

Simon's communication in this scenario was entirely adult prompted.

Scenario 2

Only two days later, after discussion with the research team, the teacher adopted a different approach in the drinks session. She had the same two transparent jugs of juice, but instead of going round the table, she stood nearby and held the two jugs up without saying anything. Nothing happened for a few moments and then Simon, seeing the drinks, stretched out his arm towards the orange.

In this scenario, when aspects of Simon's communication envi-ronment were rendered more enabling, he was quickly able to begin to communicate spontaneously. The reaching gesture he used could be developed into pointing.

Factors which may have been communication *disabling* in Scenario 1 were:

- the use of a 'going round the table' approach which encourages children simply to wait and not initiate

- too much use of speech which Simon was unlikely to understand

- too early a use of physical prompting which probably pre-empted Simon's own realization that he wanted a drink and that he could get one by initiating communication.

Strategies which were more communication-enabling in Scenario 2 were:

- use of a minimal speech approach

- no use of adult verbal prompts to elicit communication

- use of time delay to enable Simon to respond to an environmental cue (i.e. the presence of the jug of juice).

Further in-depth discussion of such enabling approaches forms a central theme of this book. This scenario also illustrates that many of the disabling aspects of the environment that we saw in our research often included approaches which are well established in many classrooms as routine practice. We will highlight the need both for greater awareness of these environmental issues and for a substantial investment in professional training so that staff can review their attitudes as well as improve their level of skill and knowledge.

Summary Points

- Spontaneous communication is vital in enabling children to begin to exert control over their environments and to develop as self-determined individuals.

- Enabling children with autism and minimal or no speech to communicate *spontaneously* should be regarded as a major educational aim.

- To gain a whole picture of children's true communication capabilities, it is necessary to explore the nature of their communication environments as well as the children's abilities.

- Environments provided by staff can be disabling for these children. Adequately financed professional training that examines attitudes as well as skills and knowledge will be needed to alter this situation.

- To gain a whole picture of children's communication capabilities, it is necessary to explore the nature of their communication environments and the extent to which they are enabling or disabling.

2

The Research
Approaches and Findings

Background To The Research
Children in the Study

Eighteen children aged between two and six took part in our study. All of the children had a previous diagnosis of autism from experienced professionals and these diagnoses were further verified through the use of the Childhood Autism Rating Scale (Schopler, Reichler and Renner 1988). All of the children were communicating at an early level with only two children using single words to communicate. The other children did not speak but used a range of other prelinguistic means of communicating, including moving an adult's hand, vocalizing or pointing. The children were based in five classrooms, four of which were specifically for children with autism, in five different special schools in the UK.

Practitioners in the Study

Teachers known to have a particular interest in developing their practice in the area of communication agreed to take part in the research. Classroom assistants in the study classrooms participated in a number of ways and four speech and language therapists working in the study schools also took part.

What Did We Do?

We collected information in each school over a two- to four-month period by:

- videotaping children in a specific range of everyday school situations

- recording each child's spontaneous communications for one whole school day

- interviewing teachers and speech and language therapists

- collecting information from school reports

- using a range of assessment schedules, some of which focused on the child's capabilities while others focused on the nature of their communication environment.

We were able to make suggestions for changing practice after the data had been collected. On some occasions, it was possible to videotape what happened when staff tried out these suggestions.

We also worked directly with 14 children ourselves, using video-taped Proximal Communication approaches after the shadowing data had been collected. Proximal Communication is the term Whittaker (1996) and Whittaker and Reynolds (2000) have employed to describe the use of a particular set of communication-enabling approaches, adopted within the context of 1:1 playful inter-action settings. Chapter 4 contains a detailed discussion of Proximal Communication.

Research Definitions

A key issue in the research was how spontaneous communication was to be defined. A number of definitions have been discussed. For example, Hubbell (1977) argued that utterances were spontaneous if made by the child 'on his own volition, as opposed to utterances pur-posefully elicited by the clinician' (p.216). Zanolli, Daggett and Adams (1996) stated that spontaneity occurs 'in the absence of prompts or initiations from others' (p.407).

For the purposes of our research, communication was recorded as spontaneous if it was deemed *intentional* and occurred *without verbal prompting from adults.*

Decisions about Intentionality

The ability to communicate *intentionally* constitutes a fundamental early step on the path to effective communication. Wetherby and Prizant (1989) stated that intentionality may be described as 'the deliberate pursuit of a goal' (p.77) or more specifically 'the ability to use expressive signals in a preplanned manner in order to affect the behaviour or attitudes of others' (Prizant and Wetherby 1985, p.21). In other words, when children are communicating intentionally, they are actively trying to send a message to another person which they hope the person will act on. When communication is pre-intentional, adults may attach meaning to a particular behaviour, but the children themselves are not deliberately intending to convey that message.

During the early stages of communicating, it is often not clear whether children intend their behaviour to influence others. We had to decide whether communications which children produced during observations were intentional or not. To determine this, we used Wetherby and Prizant's (1989) useful list of observable criteria, which stated that communication could be said to be intentional if any of the following behaviours were observed:

- alternation of eye gaze between the goal and the listener
- persistent signalling until the goal is achieved
- changing the communicative signal until the goal has been achieved
- awaiting a response from the listener
- displaying satisfaction if the goal is met or dissatisfaction if it is not.

An important further check on the children's intentionality was provided by the use of a standardized assessment of the children's thinking skills (Dunst 1980; Uzgiris and Hunt 1989). The children all produced intentional behaviours in the variety of problem-solving situations covered by the Dunst Scale.

Teaching children such as those in our study to communicate intentionally forms a very important early goal that is discussed further in Chapter 4.

Ethical Approaches to Research with Children with Autism

Increasingly, researchers are becoming aware of the need to empower children participating in research through serious consideration of their rights and needs at all stages of the process (Beresford 1997; Ward 1996).

We were particularly concerned with two key ethical points. First, we believed that participation in the research should be as *enjoyable* and *meaningful* as possible for the children involved. To achieve this aim, we adopted a number of child-led approaches (see Chapter 4, for example). Second, we wanted children to benefit directly from their involvement and sought to ensure this by providing detailed feedback on research findings to teachers and parents within two to four months of completing data collection in their school.

Data Analysis

We used a number of approaches to data analysis, which are described in the Appendix. Analysis of the communication environment was undertaken from the videotapes, using the Analysing the Communicative Environment (ACE) Inventory (Rowland and Schweigert 1993).

Key Research Findings

1. All of the children in the study communicated spontaneously to some extent.

2. What the children communicated and how much they communicated depended to a significant degree on the nature of their communication environments.

These form the overall findings from the study. Below we explore various aspects of these findings in more detail.

The Children's Spontaneous Communication: Findings

This section focuses on aspects of the children's spontaneous communication: how often they communicated spontaneously; what they communicated about; where they communicated and whom they communicated with.

Rates of Spontaneous Communication

- The rate and quality of communication did not depend on a child's age, degree of autism, degree of additional impairments, adaptive behaviour score, or classroom staffing ratios (Whittaker and Potter 1999b).
- Levels of spontaneous communication were directly related to the nature of the wider communication environment, not to the degree of the child's impairment *per se*.

It is very important to observe that the rate and quality of the children's spontaneous communication does not appear to have been a characteristic of their autism *per se*. If it were, then one would expect to see most communication from children whose autism was less severe, and this was not the case. The strong implication, therefore, is that their spontaneous initiations were related, to some extent, to factors within their communication environments.

Purpose of the Children's Spontaneous Communication

- Shadowing data revealed that the purpose of the majority of the children's communications were requests and/or reject/protests.

This finding is in agreement with Wetherby's (1986) discussion of the order in which communicative functions appear in the development of children with autism, beginning with request and reject. Teaching request and reject or protest form appropriate early goals for these children. Communicating for the purposes of sharing attention or asking for information are functions that some children with autism may develop later on.

- Statistically significant relationships existed between the overall number of communications and the number of requests and protests during shadowing. Those children who requested most communicated most overall. Those who requested least communicated least overall and most of their communications were protests (Whittaker and Potter 1999b).

The relationship between request and overall levels of communication is an interesting and potentially important one. The implication is that these aspects of the children's communication did not occur together by chance. It could be argued that children who often make requests are well motivated by their environment and therefore initiate communication often. This is an issue that clearly warrants further exploration in future research.

Communicative Partners

- Shadowing data showed that almost all communications were directed towards familiar adults.

- A small number of spontaneous communications were directed towards other children with autism on shadowing days and on other videotaped occasions.

Most of the classmates of the children in our study also have autism. The possibility of interaction between children with autism has often been thought to be extremely unlikely (Berkell 1992) because of the significant difficulties which each child experiences in the area of socialization and communication. The fact that some children did interact with their classmates is interesting and again of potential significance. Approaches identified as being successful in enabling children with autism to begin to communicate with each other are discussed in Chapter 8.

Ways of Communicating

- The data revealed that the children in our study used a wide range of communicative behaviours to convey their messages.

- The two most frequently used means of communication were physical manipulation, that is physically moving part of another person (19 per cent of all spontaneous communications) and re-enactment, that is performing part or all of a behaviour sequence associated with a desired outcome (12 per cent of all spontaneous communications). A typical example of re-enactment was when children rotated both hands, wanting the teacher to sing 'Wind the Bobbin Up'.

- Five children used pointing to communicate. Four of these children had been taught to do so and two of them pointed at relatively high rates.

- Two children used multipointing (Potter and Whittaker 1997) having been taught to do so. Multipointing is where children point more than once in sequence to communicate a single message. Using multipointing, these children expressed the most complex messages of all of the children in the study.

These findings indicate that children with autism do want to communicate with others and use a number of communication behaviours to do so. Possible approaches to the rapid introduction of conventional communication systems are discussed in Chapter 6.

Contexts for Communication: Individual and Group Work

- Shadowing and video analysis revealed that most spontaneous communications occurred in 1:1 sessions. However, high levels of spontaneous communication were sometimes observed in some small group sessions where one adult worked with three or four children, using a range of communication-enabling strategies.

It is clear that the expert use of 1:1 teaching sessions with young children with autism is a necessary and powerful tool for enabling them to develop communication and social abilities (Christie *et al.* 1992; Dawson and Galpert 1990). However, given that it is generally neither possible nor always advisable for children to have unlimited access to individual teaching, it seems important that they are able to develop communication skills within the context of small group settings as well. Learning in groups, of course, also provides invaluable opportunities for children to relate to their peers. In such sessions, some practitioners in our study skilfully employed a range of communication-enabling strategies, including the presentation of appropriate communication opportunities within well-paced, predictable and comprehensible activities. Chapter 9 discusses strategies that were found to be successful in enabling children to communicate spontaneously in small group situations.

The Communication Environment: Findings

This section explores both those aspects of the children's communication environment which influenced their ability to communicate spontaneously and those that did not.

The Effects of Spoken Language

- When adults used everyday, relatively complex speech, the children in the study often withdrew from social interactions by turning away, protesting or by apparently disconnecting from the situation, which one adult called 'switching off'.

- When adults used minimal and concrete speech, with other enabling strategies, often children became more socially engaged.

These findings suggest that poor understanding and reaction to complex speech may form *part* of the reason why some children with autism withdraw from social situations. Chapter 3 discusses this important issue in more depth.

Proximal Communication:
A Communication-enabling Approach

- In videotaped 1:1 sessions where Proximal Communication techniques were used, frequencies of spontaneous communications were significantly higher than in other types of sessions. Sometimes the adults in the sessions were researchers who were much less familiar to the children, but the children still communicated at significantly higher levels than in non-Proximal Communication sessions. Proximal Communication is a particular set of communication-enabling approaches adopted within the context of 1:1 playful interaction settings, in which a minimal speech approach is emphasized.

These findings lend further weight to the argument that low rates of spontaneous communication are not necessarily an immutable characteristic of the communication profile of children with autism who have minimal or no speech. We found that the same children who communicated infrequently in some situations, communicated very frequently in others, particularly in Proximal Communication sessions. The role of Proximal Communication is discussed further in Chapter 4.

The Role of Prompting

- When adults reduced spoken prompts and paused at critical moments during an interaction or activity, children began to communicate more often and more spontaneously.

Enabling children to become communicators rather than responders involves helping them to communicate in response to environmental cues, in other words to what is happening around them. This issue is discussed further in Chapter 5.

Communication Opportunities

- Children who received frequent opportunities to communicate communicated at higher rates than those who did not.

The type and frequency of communication opportunity engineered for children was a very important factor in the creation of a communication-enabling environment. Further detailed findings and implications for practice are discussed in Chapter 7.

The Effect of Staffing Ratios

- Children's rates of communication were not related to overall staff ratios in classrooms.

In general terms, the staffing ratio in all the classrooms was high, and rightly so to meet the complex needs of this group of children, Nevertheless there was some variation, but there was no significant relationship between the staffing ratio and the rate or type of children's spontaneous communication (Whittaker and Potter 1999b). Other factors were important, such as the number and type of communication opportunities available to children over the course of the day. In other words, it was *what staff did* in terms of creating a communication-enabling environment that resulted in higher rates of communication, rather than the particular staffing ratio. We are not suggesting however that staffing levels should be decreased, rather that staff should be deployed more effectively in some classrooms. Ways in which this can be done are discussed in greater depth in later chapters.

The ACE (Analysing the Communication Environment) Analysis

We wanted to explore further the relationship between how much children communicated spontaneously and the nature of their communication environments in school. To do so, we used the Analysis of the Communication Environment (Rowland and Schweigert 1993), an assessment tool that allows teachers or speech and language therapists to analyse the overall communication value of individual activities for children with communication impairments. It focuses largely, therefore, on aspects of the communication environment rather than on the abilities of individual children. The aspects of the activity analysed by the ACE are:

- the activity (including children's enjoyment of it)

- the student's communication system

- adult interaction

- group dynamics

- materials

- specific opportunities for communication.

Not all of the sections will be appropriate for every activity. For example, in a 1:1 Proximal Communication session, the sections Group Dynamics and Materials will not be relevant.

We analysed a number of videotaped activities for each classroom using the ACE Inventory. Activities included drinks sessions, 1:1 activities and group work, with 10-minute sessions chosen at random from the videotape available. A score giving an indication of the degree to which the activity under review was communication enabling was obtained for each session by two raters and acceptable levels of agreement were found.

1. Children found to have the highest rates of spontaneous communication during shadowing days attended classrooms with the highest ACE scores. This relationship was statistically significant (Whittaker and Potter 1999b).

2. While children in all classrooms clearly enjoyed participating in many of the activities analysed, adults created deliberately engineered opportunities for communication in a minority of sessions in some classrooms.

3. Most opportunities for communication were provided during 1:1 playful interaction sessions.

4. In a number of sessions, speech used by adults seemed too complex for children to understand easily.

It is important to note that although it is essential that children enjoy activities, enjoyment in itself is not sufficient to enable them to become able communicators. It is necessary for adults to engineer frequent and high quality opportunities for children to communicate within these activities. Chapter 7 explores this issue in depth.

Summary Points

- Spontaneous communication occurs when children communicate intentionally, and without verbal, physical or gestural prompting, in response to either something happening in the environment or to some perceived internal need or want.

- All of the children in our study communicated spontaneously to some extent.

- The rate and quality of the children's spontaneous communication was not related to their degree of autism, degree of learning difficulty, chronological age or adaptive behaviour score, or to staffing ratios in the classrooms.

- Factors in the children's communication environment were found to influence the nature and frequency of their spontaneous communication.

3

A Minimal Speech Approach

Poor response to spoken language is accepted as one of the strongest indicators of early autism in very young children (Lord and Paul 1997). In this chapter, we explore the effects of different types and levels of spoken language on the children in our study and provide practical guidelines for adopting a minimal speech approach.

Key Research Findings

1. All of the children in our study experienced severe difficulties understanding speech in both everyday settings and in assessment situations.

2. Many children often appeared to withdraw from interactions with adults, with some showing aversive reactions, because they could not understand adult speech.

3. Our interview, shadowing and video data indicated that the children in our study communicated more, and did so more spontaneously, when a minimal speech approach was used.

These findings concur with a growing body of literature that identifies severe difficulties in understanding speech as a key issue for particular groups of children with autism. For example, in an overview of the communication of children with autism, Rapin and Dunn (1997) suggested that some non-verbal children might experience such severe difficulties in understanding speech that they may be said to experience 'word deafness', although they do not provide any data to support this view. Only a few studies have provided evidence on how children with autism respond to different types of speech. In one such study Peterson *et al.* (1995) concluded that there might be a group of children with autism who are 'at high risk for problems with spoken input' (p.99). Klin (1991) arrived at similar conclusions, demonstrating that children with autism showed no preference for tapes of clear maternal speech over a babble of sound in which no clear words could be distinguished. Significantly, he hypothesized that these children's lack of attraction to speech sounds may be a contributory factor to their overall social unresponsiveness.

Assessing Comprehension

Practitioners in our study agreed that it was difficult to assess exactly what children could understand in terms of the spoken word. Indeed, Schuler, Prizant and Wetherby (1997) stated that it is easy to overestimate how much speech children with autism understand because of their use of situational cues and ability to memorize daily routines.

Informal observation in familiar settings was believed by practitioners to be the most effective means of assessing children's comprehension of speech. One speech and language therapist explained her assessment approach, emphasizing that it was most productive to watch children at times of the day when there would be lots of changes in activity and therefore lots of verbal demands:

> I will actually follow [the children] round the classroom for an hour or so at key times of the day – starting with the ball pool – you can see how they respond to speech like 'ball pool' – do they go to the door? If teachers show them a ball, do they go to the door? Or is it because they see other children lining up that they go to the door?

Several members of staff emphasized the importance of the parental contribution in assessing all aspects of the children's communicative capabilities. One speech and language therapist commented: 'I find that parents often have keys to the level that the children are functioning at.' Staff also highlighted the need to distinguish between what speech children understand in well-known contexts, compared to speech understood outside these contexts. For example, a child might respond appropriately to the request 'shoes off' before going into soft play, but fail to understand the same language if told 'shoes off' at another time, for example, before a footprint painting session.

In formal assessments of language, none of the children scored on the British Picture Vocabulary Scale (Dunn *et al.* 1982) and responses to real objects such as a ball, cup, spoon (Reynell 1977) were rarely beyond chance levels.

Contextual Understanding of Speech

Many staff believed that children in the study understood speech at only a single word level and that invariably this understanding was achieved only with the additional aid of a range of contextual cues. For example, when discussing David's comprehension of speech, one speech and language therapist said:

> He seems able to respond to a number of key familiar single words, although if you were to take him into a different context he would be quite lost, but in the situations he's familiar with – he does recognize some single word vocabulary.

A teacher talking about the comprehension abilities of another child said:

> A lot of his understanding is very situational...he will now sit in circle time for longer...but if I say to him 'Alan stand up' he'd be unlikely to respond to that...you know I have to gesture – I'd probably have to give him a physical prompt to stand up and if he realizes that everyone's going to the door and getting their coats on at playtime – he sometimes might take that as a cue for getting his own coat on and go in that direction.

Additionally, and we would suggest very importantly, two teachers believed that children seemed to be *actively trying to avoid listening to speech*. One teacher said:

> I think they must often just tune out from voices, speech and voices, they must hear them around them all the time – I find it's almost as if they are just permanently tuned out from them.

Such insightful observations were supported by extensive video and shadowing data.

Practitioner Approaches to Aiding Children's Understanding of Speech

The repetition of everyday routines was believed to be important in enabling children in our study to understand what was happening in their environment. Practitioners also agreed that children generally needed additional visual and contextual cues to help them understand speech, such as the use of objects of reference, photographs or symbols. One speech and language therapist said:

> It's very much a question of getting to know how they're actually taking in information – we do know that autistic children are very good visually and they do take information in visually.

This professional went on to discuss the general effects of the use of visual cues on children's responses:

> Certainly…we have seen quite a dramatic change in behaviour from just using verbal language to then using visual clues – the calming down of the behaviour is so dramatic.

Another speech and language therapist talked about parental reports of the use of objects of reference at home, where children might bring a bottle of bath bubbles to indicate that they want a bath, for example. Most participants agreed that only very limited speech should be used with the children in our study. The notion of using 'key words' when addressing children was generally believed to be a crucial one. One teacher spoke about staff use of language as follows:

> Our strategies are to use functional language related to the situation so if it's drinks time it's 'drink, cup, juice, biscuit' those are the key words that we use.

This emphasis on functionality in the area of communication is an important one. Wetherby and Prizant (1992) emphasized that communication goals should be chosen on the basis of functional criteria, that is they should relate to abilities which will be useful in the children's everyday environments. In terms of comprehension, priority should be given to words relating to key aspects of children's everyday experiences.

Speaking to Children in Practice

Despite the fact that the nature of adult speech is recognized as very important, little research has been undertaken to explore how adults, in reality, do talk to these children in everyday settings. Konstantareas, Mandel and Homatidis (1988) found that mothers of children with autism used shorter phrases with less verbal children than did fathers, although what constituted a shorter phrase was not specified, nor how children responded to them.

In our study staff members stressed the importance of *only* using key words with children, while also acknowledging that in practice it was often difficult to adopt such an approach consistently. Both video and field notes confirmed that often quite complex speech was addressed to children by staff who had acknowledged the need for minimal speech. For example: 'That's a nice stripey top you're wearing today, isn't it, is it new?'

There may be a number of reasons for such relatively complex use of speech. For example, some adults may mistakenly believe that children understand such language when, in fact, the children are mainly responding to contextual cues rather than to the speech itself. Others may employ such running commentaries to convey a warm and caring attitude to children (Jordan and Powell 1995). We would agree that such sentiments are absolutely necessary and highly commendable in the education of all children, but our data suggest that children with autism and very limited receptive language abilities are much more likely to respond socially where warmth and concern are conveyed in essentially non-verbal ways.

Children's Response to a Minimal Speech Approach

We observed some excellent practice in what we have termed 'a minimal speech approach', where only single or two words were used consistently and appropriately in the majority of interactions with children. Where such an approach was evident, children were more socially responsive, communicated more and did so more spontaneously. Box 3.1 details the positive effects of a switch to a minimal speech approach part way through an interaction.

Box 3.1

Practice Scenario: A Minimal Speech Approach During a Trampolining Session

Setting the scene

- Janet, a classroom assistant, was working with Paul during a physical activity session on a trampoline.

- Janet was using relatively complex speech – for example, 'What are we going to do now? Shall we jump up and down a bit?'

Effects on Child Communication

- Paul was often looking away as Janet spoke and he did not attempt to initiate communication with her.

Suggestions for Change

- During the session, the researchers made two separate suggestions for change: first, that Janet should stop talking to Paul and second that she should start to imitate his vocalizations instead, which she did.

Effects of the Change on Paul's Communication

- Paul immediately began to look at Janet more.

- The number of his vocalizations increased, especially when she imitated him.

- He began to vocalize to initiate interaction with Janet within less than a minute.

Benefits of the Changed Approach

- Janet's use of a minimal speech approach with Paul had immediate results.
- The session immediately became more child-led.
- Because Janet was talking less, Paul had more time and space to communicate himself.
- When Janet reverted to a more complex speech approach, the change in Paul's behaviour was again very marked. He withdrew from the interaction by turning and pulling away.

Aversive Reactions to Complex Speech

In certain situations, some children in our study appeared to have an aversive reaction to complex speech, particularly in close, face-to-face interactions and when adults were in close proximity to the child. Many staff seemed to have an intuitive grasp of this difficulty, rarely attempting to speak to children in face-to-face situations, doing so instead from the side or just behind children. In marked contrast to this aversive reaction to complex speech, children often became very responsive to face-to-face interaction in Proximal Communication sessions where the adult used no speech and imitated the children's vocalizations or engaged in pause-burst exchanges (see Chapter 4).

Key Characteristics of a Minimal Speech Approach

The findings described above, together with detailed analysis of video and observational data, demonstrated that the ways in which adults talked to children often significantly affected their communication and social responses.

We believe that the use of a minimal speech approach is important in the creation of a more communication-enabling environment for children such as those in our study, to ensure that they do not disengage from their social environment because they cannot understand that spoken environment.

Modifying the linguistic environment of children with autism is by no means a novel suggestion. Curcio and Paccia (1987) found that the responsiveness of mainly verbal children with autism increased when features of adult conversation were conceptually simplified and when 'Wh' questions were avoided. Lord (1985) suggested that a modified linguistic approach, consisting of shortening sentences, limiting gestures and limiting vocabulary, might enable children with autism to understand more of their spoken environment. In addition to such general suggestions, we believe that more explicit and practice-orientated guidelines are necessary to support the transfer of a minimal speech approach from theory to practice and in everyday situations. Key characteristics of the approach are detailed below.

Reducing the Use of Speech in All Situations

When interacting with children with significant difficulties in understanding speech, the use of single words or very short (2–3 word) functional phrases in as many situations as possible is very likely to increase children's levels of engagement. Such an approach, in conjunction with strategies such as the use of visual cues and adult use of pointing and multipointing, is likely to enable children to progress in their understanding of individual words.

Appropriate Mapping of Single Words

Adults need to be careful to map words *exactly* onto aspects of the situation in hand. Unhelpful mismatches can sometimes occur when children do produce communications. For example, at drinks time when a child chooses a drink, an adult may say 'good boy', understandably wanting to praise the child for his effort. A more comprehensible and effective thing to do, from the child's point of view, would be to say 'drink' clearly and emphatically at the relevant moment.

Another potentially inappropriate, though understandable language focus, may relate to an emphasis on social routine words such as 'please' or 'thank you'. Such concepts are very difficult for some children with autism to understand because of their abstract nature. These are phrases that would only be appropriate to emphasize in children's communication environments when it was clear that they understood a very wide range of object names, concrete action names and functional everyday requests.

It is important that the words we say to children who experience severe difficulties in understanding speech, relate directly to the most concrete and relevant focus of their attention. If a child's attention is clearly focused on a crisp being handed over, it's important to say 'crisp' at that moment. It is only by trying to ensure that words are mapped *exactly* onto the most relevant aspect of the children's experience at any given moment that they are likely to begin to associate specific words with specific concepts.

It appeared, from our observations, that the speed and intonation used, even with single words, was an important factor in the children's understanding. Clear, slow pronunciation of each syllable, with an emphasized pattern of intonation, appeared to be most effective. This aspect of a minimal speech approach should be investigated further in future research. The use of intonation in phrases is considered below. We observed that, in general, classroom teams found it easier to map speech onto appropriate aspects of a situation when engaged in relatively structured activities, where the situation itself suggested specific language. For example, when independent tasks were completed, adults generally said *only* the word 'finished'. It is important to be able to map speech onto salient aspects of less structured situations. For example, when walking with children to assembly, relevant speech might be 'hall now', supported by a photograph, rather than saying, 'It's time for assembly, we're all going to the hall now.' Any speech used will be much more effective and comprehensible if it relates to the here and now in a very concrete and direct way.

Giving Information in Non-verbal Ways

Giving information to children with autism using a visual format has long been advocated (Koegel and Wilhelm 1973), but in practice adults may often continue to use more speech than is necessary while at the same time using visual cues. For example, an adult may show a child a picture of the toilet but also say, 'Come on, off we go to the toilet now.' Such relatively complex speech may actually distract the child from being able to understand the cue given by the picture. Furthermore, the child has little chance of understanding the speech separate from the picture. In this situation, the use of the single word 'toilet' would be more effective.

Another non-verbal way of giving information is to use gesture or multipointing (Potter and Whittaker 1997). For example, when asking children to put their gym shoes into a bag, instead of saying 'Could you put your pumps into the bag, please', the adult could point first to the shoes and then to the bag, only later mapping single words onto the situation once children have understood what is required.

Trying to Minimize 'Running Commentary' Approaches

When interacting with children with autism who have little or no speech, it can be challenging to establish the sort of flowing interaction that we, as fluent communicators, feel most comfortable with. Providing a running spoken commentary on what is happening is a strategy that might help us to 'fill in the gaps' and establish some sort of continuity within the interaction. However, speech tends to become complex during such commentaries and, as discussed above, may cause some children with autism to disengage from the social situation. Adults need to be aware of this and are likely to find that other non-speech based approaches will be more successful in engaging such children in social interactions. Practical suggestions for how this may be achieved are given in Box 3.2.

Box 3.2

Practice Scenario: Going Out to Play

In less structured situations, such as getting ready to go out to play, adults may understandably slip into using more complex speech such as 'Let's go and get your coat on now, ready for playtime'. Unfortunately, some children with autism are unlikely to understand such phrases and may disengage from the situation. It would be more effective to show such children a picture of a coat and say only 'coat'. Social interaction between the adult and child could be better achieved, in this situation, by playing a simple game when the child's coat is on – for example, a peek-a-boo or tickling game.

Practice Scenario: Interacting with Children on a Walk

Another unstructured scenario, where the consistent use of a minimal speech approach might prove challenging for adults to maintain, is while out walking, to the shops or local playground, for example. Are there more comprehensible ways of engaging children as you walk without using complex speech?

One classroom teacher in our study used the idea of event strips, which contained computer-generated symbols representing each stage of the walk. Books of photographs in sequence can also be used. Small photo albums with one picture per page are ideal. It is vital to check that children understand these pictures or representations.

Another teacher used nursery rhymes as an enjoyable and meaningful way of engaging young children in a social activity while walking. She paused at the end of lines, waiting for children to indicate in some way that they wanted her to continue singing.

Delaying the Use of Speech When Teaching New Tasks

When attempting to teach a new task to children with autism who have severe receptive language difficulties, it is likely to be much more effective to demonstrate the task using little or no speech until children understand what is required. Later, when they are familiar with the task, appropriate single words can be mapped onto relevant aspects of the situation.

In many situations, the intellectual aspect of a task will be much easier for these children to understand than the spoken language aspect of the instruction to perform that task. The example in Box 3.3 details a non-verbal way of teaching during a computer session.

Box 3.3

Practice Scenario: Minimal Speech
During a Computer Session

An adult might instruct a child to use the mouse, during a computer session, by saying 'move the mouse and press the button'. Such speech may be too complex for some children with autism and may distract them from understanding what is required. It is certainly unlikely to help them to understand what they must do.

A more effective way of enabling the child to understand the task would be to model the action and then physically prompt the child to do the same, without using any speech. This would demonstrate the cause and effect nature of what is happening. Later, as children become familiar with what they have to do, the adult may use the key word 'press', either as an instruction to the child or as a comment when the child presses the button. In this case, the child is only being asked to process one piece of information at a time. The teaching prompt is a non-verbal model and only later, when the child has mastered the skill, is the key word associated with the action.

Avoiding a Focus on Relative Terms such as Here, There,
Mine, Yours, This, That, Big, Little, In or On

Such abstract terms are very difficult for some children with autism to understand since their meaning is relative, being neither fixed nor concrete. As adults, we use these terms very frequently in everyday speech and therefore rarely think about how complex and relative they are. Such concepts are very unlikely to form an appropriate early focus in communication teaching for children such as those in our study.

Avoiding Temporal Terms such as Yesterday, Tomorrow as Early Comprehension Goals

Again, temporal terms, such as 'today, tomorrow, before, after, now, later' are similarly abstract and therefore difficult to understand. However, of these terms, 'later' can be one of the most useful. It was used very effectively in one of our study classrooms to indicate that children could undertake a spontaneously requested activity later in the day but not immediately. Terms such as 'now' and 'later' can be taught using sequences of pictures as within a structured teaching format (Schopler 1995), as well as within the daily routines of the classroom.

Examples of a Minimal Speech Approach

In Table 3.1 we compare the use of an everyday speech approach with a minimal speech approach in a range of routine classroom scenarios.

Table 3.1 Comparison of everyday speech with minimal speech approach		
Situation	**Everyday Speech**	**Minimal Speech Approach**
Asking what children want to drink	An adult holds up two bottles of juice in front of a child with autism and severe difficulties understanding speech and says 'Do you want orange or apple juice?' If the child doesn't respond quickly the adult says, 'Which one do you want, the orange or apple?'	An adult holds up two bottles of juice in front of the child and does not say anything. If the child does not respond, after a reasonable pause, the adult takes his finger and prompts him to point to one of the bottles, again without speaking. Later, when the communicative exchange is established, she may say 'drink' as the child chooses one.

Telling children it's time for soft play	An adult shows the child a photograph of the soft play room and says, 'Look Helen, it's time to go to the soft play room, so you need to take your shoes off.'	The adult shows the child a photograph of the soft play room and says 'soft play' as the child is looking at it and leads her to the chairs where the children normally take off their shoes before the soft play session, without saying anything further.
Children are having difficulty taking shoes off	An adult approaches a child and says, 'What's the matter Peter? Are you stuck? Do you want me to help you? You need to ask me to help you.'	The adult approaches a child and takes his hand and physically prompts him to point to her and then to the shoes. She might say nothing or just 'shoes' as the child points to the shoes.

Identifying Children with Severe Difficulties Understanding Speech

It is obviously essential to be able to identify accurately those children experiencing extreme difficulties understanding speech. This is a complex undertaking in which multi-professional teams need to work closely together to harmonize their expertise. As stated earlier, very careful observation is needed to ascertain whether children are actually responding to speech itself, rather than to other contextual cues. Alternatively, there may be a degree to which children's lack of response to speech may be attributed to their autism and/or general unwillingness to comply with instructions. For children with autism and minimal or no speech, however, it could well be that such unresponsiveness or even withdrawal may be a direct result of their severe inability to understand spoken language. Key questions for revealing children's problems in understanding speech might be:

- Do you nearly always need to repeat spoken requests?

- Do you nearly always need to help certain children to understand what you have said by demonstrating what has to be done or by taking them to the right place?

- Has a hearing loss been suspected? It is crucial to check whether children *are* experiencing any actual difficulties in hearing (see below).

- Do some children often seem to have a 'blank' expression when being spoken to?

- Does the child often turn away or try to leave the situation when being spoken to?

- Does the child respond more positively when little or no speech is used?

One approach to the issue of disentangling the effects of the children's autism from their difficulties in understanding speech would be systematically to compare their response to verbal as opposed to non-verbal instructions or overtures in the same situations.

The Problem of Hearing Loss

A variety of different methods are used by audiologists to assess potential hearing loss in children, depending on their level of development and their ability and willingness to co-operate. Screening assessment in young babies involves a distraction test, while with older children co-operative tests are employed, which generally require the child to understand language. If problems are detected during screening then children can be referred for auditory evoked response testing which measures the brainstem's reaction to sound.

It is difficult to screen for hearing loss in children who have autism and minimal speech. The children's difficulty in understanding language generally precludes co-operative testing so distraction tests are often employed. These involve the tester being in close proximity to the child to use special rattles or other auditory stimuli. Unless these are skilfully employed there is a real danger that the children may be aware of the presence of the tester and turn in response to them rather than the sound source. We would recommend video-taping of the screening for later slow motion analysis to help to guard against this.

In our current research we employed a distraction technique for screening hearing that we have used over a number of years. It involves transmission of a standard sound source via a miniature earpiece that is presented to the child's ear on the end of a fine rod. This equipment allows the tester to stand some distance from the child, to minimize detection, yet place the sound source near the child's ear. Sound levels are checked prior to assessment using a sound meter. Using this equipment we detected a potential problem with one child in the study who was then recommended for specialist audiological examination. There is a growing body of literature suggesting that a significant proportion of children with autism may have undetected hearing loss. We would strongly support the view of Klin (1993) that all children with autism have detailed auditory examinations. New techniques are being developed and refined which should have widespread application with children who are difficult to test (Grewe, Danhauer and Thornton 1994). Although some children with autism and minimal speech pass audiological tests, they may have more difficulty in the auditory processing of speech rather than environmental sounds.

Implementing a Minimal Speech Approach: Practice Challenges

There are likely to be a number of challenges involved in the imple-mentation of a minimal speech approach in everyday settings. As Ayres et al. (1994) highlighted, there are often legitimate difficulties for staff in the practical implementation of new approaches in the classroom. These may relate to the need to change long-held attitudes or beliefs, as well as to the actual process of changing practice itself.

Changing Attitudes

Classroom staff may have a number of valid concerns about the use of a minimal speech approach. Speech is the accepted means of communication between people, so to suggest that very limited amounts of speech should be used with some children may be to challenge deeply held assumptions about what constitutes an appropriate communication environment. For example, in one of our research feedback sessions a member of staff wondered how children could learn to speak themselves if adults did not speak fluently to them. This is a very important issue, which needs to be examined. In Table 3.2 we address this concern and a number of others which staff may express relating to the use of a minimal speech approach, together with responses to such concerns.

Table 3.2 Concerns about use of minimal speech approach	
Possible Concerns	**Suggested Responses**
The exposure issue • How will children learn to speak if we do not talk freely with them?	• Children with severe comprehension difficulties do not learn to understand speech by hearing complex everyday speech (Schopler 1995). Too much speech is very likely to confuse them and possibly cause them to disengage from their social environment (Klin 1991).
• How will children learn to understand speech if we don't talk very much to them?	• It seems possible that some children with autism who do not use speech to communicate are not able to do so because of motor programming difficulties (Prizant 1996). That is, they may have difficulties in producing the right sounds in the right order. They may also have problems in processing incoming sounds.

Speech: The Teaching Medium There is a belief that the teaching of others is achieved primarily through the use of speech.	Speech as a teaching medium is only successful for those who can understand it easily. If children find speech extremely difficult to understand, the use of a speech intensive approach is likely to be unsuccessful.
Chronological Age Concerns We should talk to children according to the age they are and not as if they were much younger.	It has been argued that communicating with children at a level which they can understand is likely to be the most respectful approach (Nind and Hewett 1994).
Affect Issues It feels quite unnatural and 'distant' talking to children in single words.	Adults can and should communicate empathy, warmth and concern but using approaches that do not involve lots of speech, for example, through Proximal Communication and imitating what children do (see Chapter 4).

Ensuring Consistency of Approach

The importance of a consistent team approach in creating an appropriate spoken environment for children such as those in our study cannot be overemphasized. We would suggest that in order to ensure such consistency, it is vital for classroom teams to have opportunities for in-depth discussion on any concerns they may have about both the introduction and maintenance of a minimal speech approach. Staff are unlikely to change their practice if they are not convinced by the rationale underlying any particular teaching strategy. Regular follow-up discussions are necessary to monitor how the team is feeling about aspects of implementation to date and how their skills in the use of the approach are progressing. The danger of regression is also present, when staff begin to slip back into more complex speech patterns after having successfully used a minimal speech approach.

Changing What We Do in Practice

There are other issues relating to the difficulty of implementing changes in practice. There is a need to explore the difference between what we say and think we do and what we actually do. For example, while the notion of using key words with individuals with communication impairments is by no means new (Howlin and Rutter 1987; Owens and Rogerson 1988), the implementation of such an approach remains problematic in everyday school environments for a number of reasons, as indicated above.

First, it is not necessarily easy for fluent users of speech substantially to reduce their spoken language when working with children such as those in our study. In addition, interacting with children using minimal speech may understandably feel 'unnatural' to begin with. Furthermore, within the context of a busy classroom, it may be difficult to assess exactly how much speech is being used with particular children. Several of our participants were surprised at how much speech they did use when watching video clips of their own practice.

It is clear that classroom teams require support and guidance to reflect on their practice in this complex area. In order to achieve a minimal speech approach, adults will need to find effective ways of monitoring the spoken language environment. Initial training will be vital to ensure that all relevant staff understand what is being advocated and why. In particular, the notion of what constitutes a minimal speaking approach must be clearly explained, demonstrated and agreed. A clearly written statement detailing what the approach is and the rationale for using it should be prepared (see Chapter 10 for an example).

Discussion centred on video clips of their classroom practice may be useful in helping adults become aware of how much speech they are using. The use of video in staff training, however, needs careful handling to ensure that staff feel supported during this process and that professional self-esteem is preserved. (See Potter and Richardson 1999 for a discussion of guidelines on the use of video workshops in staff training.)

When adults do use key words (one, two or three words) consistently, in context and combined with an initial use of visual cues or objects of reference, it is clear that children such as those in our study can learn to understand some speech. One teacher reported that she no longer needed to use pictures to support some words because she felt children could now understand the word alone, in context. Such understanding, however, is much less likely to be achieved if key words are buried within longer phrases, even where the phrases are only five or six words long.

Coping with Different Receptive Ability Levels in a Class

Another possible challenge to the implementation of a minimal speech approach is that there is often a wide range of receptive language abilities within a single class. Some children may be able to understand relatively complex speech, which may cause problems in whole class situations. For example, many classrooms use the notion of circle times to foster a sense of group identity. The need for the use of a minimal speech approach with some children, however, may mean that such sessions need to be reconsidered. Children in our study often appeared to 'switch off' or protest during sessions where complex speech was being used to benefit children in the class who could understand it.

It may be better, in some sessions, to divide groups of children according to how much speech they can understand. An alternative session for whole class work might be to structure a group musical activity, since some children with autism seem to respond better to singing than the spoken word, as is discussed later in this chapter. One such successful session we observed involved the singing of the 'Hello' song in which children passed a hat, necklace, toy glasses, scarf, etc. around the circle to show whose turn it was. The items passed provided a concrete cue for the children as to what was happening, as well as indicating when the song would be finished. Such a session was enjoyable, as well as meaningful to all of the children involved.

A Minimal Speech Approach for How Long?

During one of our feedback sessions a participant asked how long it might be necessary to use a minimal speech approach. There is almost no long-term information on what happens to the comprehension of children such as those in our study over time. Peterson *et al.* (1995) found that the comprehension abilities of the two children in their study had not improved one year after the initial research. They suggested that for some children with autism, very poor understanding of spoken language might constitute a relatively stable characteristic over time. This is an area that requires greater exploration. As we reported earlier, some children in our study did appear to understand more speech over time, where single words were used consistently, in context and with the support of pictures or objects of reference. Practitioners will obviously be guided by their own observations as to when children no longer need pictorial cues, as well as the spoken word, to convey messages to them. The best way to decide this may be through the use of mini-experiments in naturally occurring situations. If children consistently respond to the spoken word on its own in the test situation, then the visual cue could probably be safely discarded.

Use of Emphasis, Rhythm and Tone in Speech

Another important issue related to how adults use spoken language with children with autism concerns the potential beneficial effects of repetitious and rhythmical speech. Prevezer (1990) discussed this issue within the context of the Music Assisted Communication Approach.

It was extremely noticeable that many of the children in our study responded positively to counting activities where an adult pointed to pictures or objects and slowly and rhythmically counted to five or ten. Some children actually prompted members of staff to count by pointing to the number and then looking at the adult, waiting for her to say the number. Interestingly, this was one of the few occasions when children in the study were observed *to ask adults to say words*. One reason for this could be that the words for numbers always come in a predictable sequence and are usually spoken with an exaggerated lilting intonation. Also, when counting adults tended to slow speech down very considerably. Equally interesting was the observation that a few children who did not use speech to communicate were nevertheless able to count to five or ten using speech. These issues are clearly worthy of further exploration.

As a general issue, the practice points emerging from the above discussion may be that adults should try to use as much exaggerated intonation in their speech as possible, in appropriate contexts. The scenario in Box 3.4 provides an excellent example of such an approach.

Box 3.4

Practice Scenario: Exaggerated Storytelling

Exaggerated use of intonation was put to very good effect in one classroom that had daily story-time sessions. Children in our study were very attentive during the telling of stories such as 'What's the Time Mr Wolf?' and Rod Campbell's 'Oh Dear, No Eggs Here' when they were told in a very slow, repetitious way, with greatly exaggerated use of intonation. All staff in the room almost chanted the stories together, thus adding to the drama of the situation. Although it is very doubtful that the children in our study were able to understand the majority of the actual words and concepts in the stories, yet they did respond very positively to the way in which the stories were told and, in particular, to the climactic nature of the storylines. They were thus able to enjoy participating in a relatively large group session. The teacher who used this approach said:

> I think that the way I tell a story is very, very expressive...you know my voice is expressive...my body language is expressive...I'm wanting them to anticipate and to be interactive with me in the story – I think I am a lot more *emphatic* in my voice – I try and keep my voice very clear.

How can we account for this positive response to what must be termed a complex spoken language situation? One possible answer may relate to the purpose and prosodic aspects of adult speech in this specific context. Adults were using speech in these story sessions to convey anticipation and excitement to children, who *did not need to understand the precise meaning of individual words* to participate. Furthermore, as we have seen, speech was slow, repetitious and rhythmical. In other complex speech situations, children may be expected to understand the actual words themselves and prosodic scaffolding may be lacking: for example, when an adult says 'it's time to go to the ball pool, you need to take your shoes and socks off', using everyday intonation, at a normal speed of delivery. Further exploration of the ways in which children with similar ability patterns respond to speech in a variety of contexts is certainly warranted.

The Benefits of Musical Approaches for Children with Autism

Related to children's reaction to rhythmical use of speech is their response to singing and music. Two practitioners in our study talked about children's heightened responses to singing as opposed to speech. One teacher said:

> William seems to understand singing more than spoken words – I don't know whether he actually does – but he certainly responds better if you sing about routines and things you're doing.

Another teacher explained:

> I use singing a lot in my approach with the children – because I often find that that is more effective than speech.

Trevarthen *et al.* (1998) referred to the extensive literature available which documents the social and communication gains which children with autism have made in response to both structured and more freely creative music therapy approaches. A number of case studies have been recorded, for example, by Alvin and Warwick (1992) and Nordoff, Robbins and Britten (1985). Prevezer (1990) provided some very practical guidelines for the use of music and song as a means of encouraging interaction between an adult and a child. A key point seems to be that music can provide very effective scaffolding, within which social interactions can begin to develop.

Summary Points

- Some children with autism experience extreme difficulties understanding speech.

- It is very easy to overestimate how much speech such children can understand because of their use of situational cues to understand their environment.

- Children with autism and severe difficulties in understanding speech may disengage from their social environment because they cannot understand that spoken environment. Some children may demonstrate aversive reactions to complex speech.

- Practitioners should try to use a minimal speech approach when talking to such children.

- We are not advocating a *no speech* approach with these children. We *are* advocating that adults use only necessary and minimal speech for as much time as possible, supporting this with visual cues or objects of reference as appropriate.

- The use of rhythmical and exaggerated patterns of intonation within speech, as well as musical approaches, can enable some children with autism to respond more positively to spoken language.

4

Proximal Communication
An Autism Specific Interactional Approach

We have applied the term Proximal Communication (Whittaker 1996) to a range of non-verbal techniques that adults can use to engage children with autism in social interactions. It involves playful exchanges, which can include rough and tumble play, tickling and imitation of the child. Short *bursts* of activity from the adult are followed by definite *pauses* to encourage the child to initiate frequent communication. Proximal Communication has its theoretical foundations in work on social interactions between adults and children in infancy (Bruner 1975; Newson and Newson 1975; Schaffer 1996).

Central to our Proximal Communication approach is a belief that children with autism and minimal speech are capable of communicating intentionally and are active partners.

Key Research Findings

1. Immediate and substantial increases in intentional communication were shown in Proximal Communication sessions by children who communicated very infrequently in other settings.

2. Children were responsive to Proximal Communication irrespective of their rate of spontaneous communication in other situations.

3. A range of communication strategies was shown by different children with a minimum of prompting from the

adult. Generally only a single strategy was used in any given communication. These included: hand signalling, where the child touched the adult's outstretched hand to restart the activity; vocalization; or eye gaze. Children who had been previously taught to point or multipoint were able to use these strategies in Proximal Communication sessions.

4.   The children appeared to enjoy the sessions as approaching the adult, and smiling, giggling or laughing generally accompanied their communications. The adult, not the child, ended most of the sessions. There is some evidence that it helps to establish affective ties, which are important in building relationships.

5.   There was evidence that the absence of adult speech was important in sustaining the Proximal Communication at such high levels.

6.   No external rewards such as sweets etc. were used, or necessary, to achieve these results.

We will illustrate these findings with two short case studies.

Box 4.1

Joe

We observed Joe, a 5-year-old child with autism and no speech, for a full school day. During that time, he communicated only 39 times – an average of 7 communications per hour. By contrast, a 2-year-old communicates around 200 times per hour (Wetherby et al. 1988). Nine of Joe's communications were to request food or objects, while the other 30 were to protest or reject actions of adults. These interactions lasted no more than a few seconds with any attempt to prolong them leading to him becoming extremely distressed.

By contrast, during a continuous 40-minute videotaped interaction session with an adult, who was using Proximal Communication strategies, Joe communicated 164 times – all of these communications were requests for social interaction, and were accompanied by laughter and appropriate eye contact.

Tony

Tony was also 5 years old with autism and minimal speech. He communicated spontaneously an average of 9 times per hour across the school day. Only three of his communications were requests for social interaction. Again, during a videotaped interaction with two adults using Proximal Communication techniques he communicated 71 times in a *four-minute* period. All of these communications were requests for social interaction.

These case studies show a remarkable increase in the frequency of social communication of the two children involved. They are not, however, isolated examples, for highly significant increases in rates of communication were shown by all of the children with whom we were able to use this approach. We had the opportunity to videotape Proximal Communication sessions with 12 out of the 18 children in the present study (67 per cent).

Proximal Communication: A Focus on Social Strengths

Proximal Communication is based upon the *social strengths* of children with autism. Whittaker (1996) and Whittaker and Reynolds (2000) pointed out that much current research, in seeking to distinguish children with autism from other matched groups, tended to focus on a *deficit model of autism*, with the deficit being located within the child. They stressed, however, that evidence for the children's *strengths* in non-verbal communication could also be found in the research literature, although it was rarely emphasized. Identified social strengths of children with autism include:

- approaching adults who were passive and not talking

- reaching out to adults after being tickled to ask for more tickling

- looking at adults after being tickled

- maintaining proximity to adults in situations where no toys or objects were being used

- a general responsiveness to 'rough and tumble' play.

These *positive* elements in the non-verbal behaviour of children with autism who have limited speech are the basis of our Proximal Communication approach.

Aims of Proximal Communication

The aim of Proximal Communication is to engage the children in playful and pleasurable non-verbal interaction to develop their early social skills. The specific communication abilities that may be developed in these sessions include the following:

- intentionality
- social timing
- spontaneous communication
- turn-taking
- social anticipation
- communicative use of eye gaze
- communicative use of vocalization
- communicative use of gesture
- responsiveness to a widening range of social games
- early stages of reciprocity
- beginnings of joint attention

Assessment Prior to Proximal Communication

Before discussing the key elements of Proximal Communication, we shall explore relevant assessment issues. The importance of making detailed observations of children in their everyday settings has been stressed throughout this book. Here we would encourage you to observe, and carefully record, the child's reactions in a variety of natural settings, particularly ones where whole body activities are involved. For example, do children like to jump, run, be spun around, do somersaults or enjoy a ride on a swing or seesaw, etc.? These observations will then inform you as to approaches that may be successful with children during Proximal Communication sessions. Note both what children do and what emotions they seem to display: enjoyment, excitement, hesitancy, etc. Settings such as soft play, ball pool, the swimming bath or paddling pool are good places to observe. Although some children like these types of vigorous activities others may be timid, or even frightened by them. Clearly we would not want to use rough and tumble play as the basis for Proximal Communication if children were uncomfortable with such an approach, so more sedentary alternatives will be discussed below.

As well as observing the child, talk to as many people as possible who know the child well, such as parents, siblings and therapists, to deepen your understanding. In the rest of this chapter we will examine the techniques used in Proximal Communication in some detail, consider important ethical questions and compare it to other approaches.

Key Elements of Proximal Communication

The various elements involved in Proximal Communication are summarized in Box 4.2. We will examine each of them in turn.

Box 4.2

Key Elements of Proximal Communication

- Positive adult attitudes: expect intentional communication, be relaxed, follow the child's interests and leads.

- Minimize your use of speech. We generally use *no speech at all*, particularly when establishing Proximal Communication.

- Use tickling and rough and tumble, appropriate to the child's physical development.

- Exaggerate facial expression and physical responses during the *active, burst phase* when you are doing something, for example, tickling.

- Contrast this active phase with a *passive, pause phase* where you remain still and watch for, and respond to, the child's attempts to communicate.

- The bigger the contrast between your reactions in the passive and burst phases, the more effective it will be.

- Decide on a key communicative response that you want to encourage from children. Eye contact is generally a good choice but some children may be more comfortable touching your outstretched hand at first.

- When children make the response, looking or touching your hand, *do not speak* but resume the active burst phase of tickling or rough and tumble.

- Shape the children's response by increasing the frequency of pauses. Don't be nervous about doing this early in the interaction. The more pauses you use, the more opportunities you create for children to communicate and the quicker they learn to do so.

- Adopt a position lower than the child's eye level, if possible.

- Imitate the children's noises or babbling.

- Use delayed echoing of the child's utterances to try to elicit imitation.

- Don't try to introduce small objects or toys, concentrate on purely interpersonal interaction. Large play equipment can sometimes help.

- Sometimes imitate the child's physical movements or actions to vary the interaction.

Positive Adult Attitudes

The adult's role in establishing the right ethos and setting for Proximal Communication is crucial, for attitudes are as important as skills. A genuine belief that the children's behaviour is intentional and that they have the right to be active participants in the communication is vital. For the approach to work the adults need to be relaxed, confident and flexible in their approach and, hopefully, enjoying the activity. They may also have to suspend some of their preconceptions about autism such as the belief, often expressed in the media, that because children have autism they do not enjoy interacting with others.

The Use of a Burst/Pause Approach to the Development of Intentional Communication

Burst/pause is a key element in Proximal Communication. Studies of one-to-one interactions between adults and babies suggest that effective adults switch between bursts of active and passive phases to allow time for the infant to respond. This burst/pause activity (Kaye 1977) has also been found to be effective with older non-verbal children with severe or profound learning disabilities (Nind and Hewett 1994; Whittaker 1984a) as well as with other children with autism who do not speak (Whittaker and Reynolds 2000).

Essentially the adult does something the child appears to enjoy – the *active, burst phase* – the adult then stops and waits – the *passive, pause phase*. The adult continues to wait for the child to communicate that he wants the activity to start again. If the child is not clearly exhibiting intentional communication, the adult treats a chosen aspect of the child's behaviour *as if it were* intentional, to help the child see the cause and effect nature of his behaviour on another person. For example, the adult may tickle the child and then wait quietly, remaining still but expectantly (large eyes and raised eyebrows), perhaps crouching in front of the child. As soon as the child happens to glance at the adult, she quickly responds with another tickle, so that the child realizes that it was the looking at the adult that caused her to repeat the action of tickling. The child becomes aware that when he looks at the adult something enjoyable happens, in this case, tickling. Once the child has realized this, then he begins to look at the adult, *expecting* that this look will have a particular effect and finally he looks in order to achieve that effect. At this stage the child can be said to be communicating intentionally in this situation.

It is particularly important that the adult responds immediately and vigorously to the behaviours he is trying to shape into an intentional signal. Within an enjoyable activity, with a skilled adult who is attentive to every detail of the child's behaviour and its possible meaning, children such as those in our study can learn to communicate intentionally surprisingly quickly. Whittaker and Reynolds (2000) argued that the behaviour is established quickly and is stable over time because it is well within the child's cognitive abilities, not because of a behavioural reinforcement effect.

We would emphasize that adults should *not speak* when the child looks at them, but that imitating the child's own vocalizations can be very effective. Some adults will find it difficult, at first, not to speak when the child looks at them, as looking is an almost universal trigger for the receiver to speak. Resist the temptation to speak and you should be able to prolong the interaction. We are currently examining the theoretical implications of this aspect of Proximal Communication.

We have found that in order for the burst/pause procedure to be effective with the children, three key elements appear to be necessary:

1. The burst phase needs to be clearly motivating to the child.

2. Transitions between the phases need to be marked by distinct contrasts in adult behaviour. So in the burst phase the adult will probably be animated in body movements and gestures and also imitating the child's vocalizations – then suddenly the adult switches into a silent, passive but responsive mode waiting for the child's communication.

3. In the pause phase, the adult needs to be prepared to wait once she knows that the child has a clearly established means of communication such as hand signalling or eye contact. *This gives the initiative to the child so that she realizes that she can communicate to get what she wants.* Some adults find

waiting difficult, but it is a crucially important part of the process.

Shaping Communication Behaviour to Reintroduce the Burst Phase

Based on their knowledge of the child, the adults must decide which behaviour they want to shape as communication. We saw, in Chapter 2, that many of the children in our study used physical manipulation of the adult to indicate requests. For example, they took the adult's hand and placed it on a desired object. This may well be accepted as a starting point because the aim of Proximal Communication is to increase the frequency of children's communication and give them the feeling of control in a social interaction scenario. One alternative that was employed very effectively by Whittaker and Reynolds (2000), as well as in the current study, is to use a hand-signalling procedure.

Hand Signalling

Following an initial burst phase the adult assumes a passive, crouched position in front of the child (the pause phase), holding out a hand at arm's length with palm vertical. If the child does not respond to the adult by touching the extended palm within around ten seconds, the adult guides the child to do so, thus demonstrating the hand-touch signal. On receiving this prompted signal, the adult starts another active phase of rough and tumble play. The adult repeats the demonstration, during a pause phase, until the child is able to use the hand-touch signal without physical prompting. Once the hand signalling is established, the adult varies her rate of responding, often pausing *after only a few seconds of activity*. In this way the child has to initiate communication frequently to maintain the interaction.

All the children in the present study who were introduced to this approach learnt it quickly, giving further support to Whittaker and Reynolds's (2000) suggestion that it is a behaviour which is well within the children's ability. It is a useful procedure because the child's intention is clear, even when viewed on videotape, and hand signalling has the potential to be linked into teaching the children to point. Its disadvantage, compared to eye contact, is that many of the children focus their attention on the adult's hand, rather than the face, so the opportunity for facial imitation is lost. Even more importantly, our long-term aim is to enable children with autism to scrutinize others' faces, for this has a fundamental role in social communication.

Adopting a Position Lower than the Child's Eye Level

Rarely did any of the adults whom we observed in this study approach the children at lower than the child's eye level. We'll call this the *low approach angle*. Adults were much more likely to bend over the children when they were attempting to communicate with them, and often this was not successful. We know from studies of non-verbal behaviour in adults that being on a higher eye level is generally perceived as a position of dominance and threat; it may be that the children find a high angle of approach uncomfortable for this reason.

Our experience suggests that a low approach angle can often be very effective in any attempt to engage a child with autism. Certainly in all the cognitive assessments which we carried out for this and our previous studies, we used the low approach angle with generally good results.

The low approach angle seems particularly effective in Proximal Communication sessions and we would say that it should be the position of first choice. If the child is standing or sitting, the adult is best crouching with one knee on the ground. If the child is sitting on the floor you may have to lie on it to maintain the angle. During the passive, pause phase of the Proximal Communication the adult should generally remain in this low angle relative to the child.

Proximity

Although this approach is called Proximal Communication we have not stressed the role of the adult's proximity to the child so far. This is because we would argue that a low approach angle and the use of burst/pause activities precede any attempt to get close to the child. Only when we have engaged the child through these two strategies would we vary the proximity.

A useful technique with some children in rough and tumble can be rapidly to approach the child when she has signalled that she wants the interaction to continue. Say 'boo' or some other explosive sound, or a brief imitation of one of the children's own sounds, as you tickle them. Then equally rapidly withdraw, returning to a passive mode in the low position waiting for the next communication.

When the interaction is quieter, then proximity may be sustained by, for example, sitting still or gently cuddling or rhythmically rocking the child. We have found that vocal interchanges may often be very effective in a quieter setting such as this.

How Rough and How Much Tumble?

Rough and tumble is a term that covers a broad range of playful inter-action behaviours generally involving large body movements and some form of physical contact. Although it is a clearly recognized aspect of children's behaviour, Pelligrini and Smith (1998) pointed out that researchers have largely neglected to examine the function of this type of physical activity play.

Observation of children prior to Proximal Communication sessions will enable the adult to make an initial judgement about how much physical activity they might enjoy. In the first example that we gave in this chapter, Joe appeared, during prior observations, to be nervous and tentative in physical activities, so the researcher worked with him on a gentle pulling game.

With other children, 'chasing' games might be more appropriate. The emphasis here isn't on running, which can be dangerous and tiring, but rather on a slow motion chase. The adult approaches the child with an exaggeratedly slow, lumbering gait, crouching and ready to pounce, building up the anticipation of the final tickle.

Adult Use of Speech

Throughout this book we have stressed the need for adults to use a minimal speech approach, that is to limit their speech to key single or two word utterances (see Chapter 3). In Proximal Communication sessions, our clear advice would be to use *no* speech at all, particularly at first. If speech is introduced later, then adhere closely to a minimal speech approach and be prepared to stop using it immediately if the child shows withdrawal behaviours. This advice is based upon our extensive experience of using these techniques over many years.

In the present study, we were able to compare the reactions of some of the children in situations where speech was used in conjunction with Proximal Communication and where the Proximal Communication was not accompanied by any speech. Some of these data came from observations of naturally occurring interactions and some from brief experimental interventions. The school personnel involved were not told in advance of what we expected to find, so that it did not influence their behaviour. One very clear example was outlined in Chapter 3 where Janet, the classroom assistant, modified her language usage and this had a significant effect on Paul's interactions. Although not all of the children reacted as dramatically as Paul, there was a clear trend for the children to disengage from the interaction when an adult began to use speech. If the speech was used in a face-to-face context, it generally produced signs of disengagement and sometimes even distress and clearly aversive reactions from some children who had been happily involved until that point. We are continuing to investigate this important finding.

You are the Major Toy

Anyone who has tried socially engaging a shy child who does not have autism knows that one method, which can be very effective, is to start playing with a developmentally appropriate new toy, in parallel with the youngster. This can draw the child into communicating with you much more effectively than if you try to interact with them directly, when they may become even more withdrawn. But children with autism find it difficult to co-ordinate their attention between an object and an adult (Lewy and Dawson 1992; Mundy and Crowson 1997). This problem with joint attention is seen as a fundamental difficulty and is one element used to differentiate children with autism from other groups. Some investigators have attempted to facilitate joint attention in experimental settings (Leekham, Hunnisett and Moore 1998), while Rosenthal Rollins *et al.* (1998) outlined an intervention technique to teach joint attention skills directly.

Our approach during Proximal Communication, which we see as complementary to direct teaching of joint attention, has been to work at a developmentally lower level, so that we are working from the child's strengths rather than their weakness. In infants one-to-one interaction between the adult and baby tends to precede joint attention. The baby appears to become skilled in the dyadic situation, before then showing the more complex behaviour of referring to a third element – the object.

Our experience in this and previous studies has been that if objects are introduced into the Proximal Communication sessions, then this is generally a distraction, as the children cannot share their attention between the adult and the object. One possible interme-diary step might be to introduce two adults into the Proximal Com-munication situation after it has been well established as an activity with the child. We have a remarkable video of Tony who was involved in a vocal interchange with Helen, a member of staff. She was imitating his vocalizations and he was looking at her and trying out different variations. Then without any prompting he approached the researcher who was videotaping the activity from across the room and began engaging him in a similar vocal exchange while also main-taining eye contact. Helen joined in, taking turns with the researcher to respond to Tony who easily switched his attention between the two adults. Tony, however, quickly took the initiative, moving between the two adults so that he was controlling who responded. We noted earlier in the chapter that he maintained this complex inter-change for four minutes and communicated 71 times in this short period. This was not, of course, an example of joint attention where the child seeks to comment to a partner about another aspect of the environment. Rather it demonstrated his ability to switch his communication from one person to another. We are currently considering ways that we might develop this activity with other children and to see if we can extend it into joint attention activities.

Using Large Play Equipment

Although we have found that small toys generally distract from the Proximal Communication interchange, some large play equipment may enhance it. Briefly activating a swing, a seesaw or pushing a child in a cart, then pausing for the child to communicate before continuing, can be effective with some children. Many years ago, we had a four-foot diameter fibreglass saucer in which the children lay and could be rapidly spun. We would then pause with the child facing us and wait for their communication to signal us to continue. It proved a popular and effective tool in promoting communication.

Vocal Imitation

Although we stressed that we would use as little speech as possible with children who had autism and no speech, we would make quite extensive use of *non-speech* vocalizations in imitation of the child's sounds. Most of the children produced vocalizations, with some making strings of sound that were analogous to infant-like babbling sequences. Babbling has been extensively studied in babies (Elbers and Ton 1985; Kimbrough, Olley and Eilers 1988; Marchman, Miller and Bates 1991) and also in young children with Down syndrome (Eilers *et al.* 1993). We hope to examine the nature of the babbling sequences produced by the children in the study in some detail at a later date to try to determine their function.

One finding to emerge from our study is that when adults imitated the children's babbling this was generally effective in engaging them in Proximal Communication routines. By using bursts of vocal imitation, followed by pauses, some children could be engaged in a non-speech vocal dialogue, with the amount of vocalization used by the children increasing significantly compared to when the adult was silent. The most prolonged example we have in the research of one of these non-speech vocal dialogues involved David and one of the researchers. The interchange lasted for 14 minutes without a break, with David producing long complex strings of non-speech vocalizations and the adult attempting to replicate them. Throughout this time David was sitting on a high cupboard, which the adult leant against so that David was slightly above and about 30 cm away. The adult tried, at times, to introduce delayed echolalia of some of David's sounds, which involved repeating vocalizations that David had used earlier in the interchange. David ignored them and continued to take the initiative with a new vocal sequence. David was familiar by this time with the researcher and had responded in a similar way some months before, but only on a single occasion that had not been videotaped.

We would suggest that a number of variations in vocal imitation can be tried, but only after a routine has been established. Try imitating a sound sequence that the child had produced earlier, as the researcher did. Here the adult is producing a babble sequence that we know the child is capable of making but which is separated in time. Does the child imitate it? Or does he respond in some other way that indicates recognition of the sound?

Alternatively, try imitating the current sound pattern, but introduce a variation by including another sound that is already in the child's repertoire. Another variation is to retain the same sound pattern but alter the pitch, so that you imitate the child's babble in a deeper or higher register.

We would emphasize that the main purpose of these activities, in the Proximal Communication sessions, is to engage children with us, *not* to teach different sound patterns. So if any of the variations caused the child to disengage we would return immediately to the original pattern. We would stress that it is important to refrain from imitating any sound patterns that are perceived as being rejections, protests or distress, and instead respond by retreating and moving into a passive phase.

Physical Imitation

Physical imitation, whereby the adult imitates the child's actions or gestures, is used quite extensively and apparently effectively in the Option programme (Trevarthen *et al.* 1998), which we discuss below. We tend to use it less frequently than vocal imitation of the children, as our subjective impression is that it is less effective in engaging them, but because of this we have less information on its use in this study. It is certainly a technique that is worth trying and, of course, it may be very effective with certain children.

Proximal Communication and Relationships

Some professionals with whom we spoke believed that, in addition to aiding early social communications skills, Proximal Communication could also help in the development of relationships. Certainly the high levels of enjoyment shown by the children make it a motivating activity for the clear majority of children with whom we have used it. From our ongoing research we have examples of children seeking us out, even after protracted gaps in our contact with them, to engage us in Proximal Communication. Clearly this is an area that would benefit from further careful evaluative research.

Settings for Proximal Communication Sessions

We have examples of effective Proximal Communication in a variety of settings – children sitting at a table, in the playground, in a quiet corner of the classroom or in a swimming pool. But our recommendation for an optimal setting would be a relatively small room, safe for rough and tumble, with the minimum of furniture and objects and with a large soft-play floor mattress. If the room is too large it could be exhausting, for the adult in particular, to play chasing games, and potentially dangerous for children if they run about too quickly. Equally a very small room could be intimidating with the child not having space to move away from the adult. One around 4 metres square (13 x 13 ft) seems ideal – or a little larger if it has fixtures such as a ball pool. Clearly, it is best if the room is familiar to the children and they associate it with pleasurable activities. A soft-play area, often with a ball pool is the room that best fits our description in most schools.

A full-length safety mirror mounted on the wall can be useful with some children – but distracting for others. So if you have one fitted then a quick, safe and effective method of covering it up is important. We found that some children would interact with the adult by watching their twin reflections, but others were diverted from the interaction by their own image in the mirror.

The essentially distraction-free environment that we have described is almost the antithesis of the stimulating environment which we generally see in schools. In the Proximal Communication setting, we want the child to focus on the interaction with the adult, not be diverted by some aspect of the material environment. However, the rest of the approaches described in the other chapters of this book take place in a full range of settings within and outside the school.

A Comparison With Other Interactive Approaches

Certain of the ideas we have outlined in this chapter will sound familiar to people experienced in the field of autism, because some aspects are employed in other intervention approaches: an understandable situation, for these techniques have a common source, being derived mainly from early child development. But there are significant differences of emphasis between Proximal Communication and other social interaction approaches that our findings suggest may be of fundamental importance. In this section we will examine similarities and differences between Proximal Communication and two other approaches: Intensive Interaction (Nind and Hewett 1994) and, first, the Option programme (Kaufman 1976).

The Option Programme

The Option Institute's approach, also known as the Son-Rise programme, is based on the work of Samahria and Barry Kaufman with their own son, Raun, who was diagnosed as having autism (Kaufman 1976, 1994). It is a child-led, one-to-one interactive approach, using a specially designed therapeutic environment. The approach stresses the need for the adult to join the child in his own world, with an attitude of complete acceptance and enthusiasm for the child's behaviours.

SIMILARITIES BETWEEN OPTION AND PROXIMAL COMMUNICATION

Both approaches are designed to engage the child in playful social interactions. Both emphasize a positive view of the child, the importance of building social relationships, and the central role of the adult as a key resource in this process of interaction.

DIFFERENCES BETWEEN OPTION AND PROXIMAL COMMUNICATION

Attitudes to Repetitive Behaviour

The Option approach emphasizes joining the child in his own world: 'We enthusiastically join in the behavior with the child. So if the child were flapping his hands, we would flap our hands along with them [sic]' (Levy 1999, p.4), thereby stressing the principle that in order to be child centred and supportive, a complete acceptance of the child's actions is necessary. By contrast, Proximal Communication emphasizes the use of non-verbal strategies, drawn from early child development, to engage the child in *reciprocal* communication. Whatever the causes of stereotyped behaviour, and they may serve different functions for different children, we would actively try to distract children and divert their attention into what we would see as more constructive activities, rather than imitating their stereotyped behaviour.

Burst/Pause

We see the careful use of the burst/pause framework in Proximal Communication as another crucially important difference. We have stressed that it is the adult who chooses a communicative behaviour (such as eye gaze) and who also dictates the pace of the interaction – introducing more pauses so that the child has to respond more frequently to maintain the interaction. The child, of course, is under no pressure to do so, nor are any external reinforcers used, such as sweets. As we have seen this produces high rates of intentional communication from the child, similar to those reported by Whittaker and Reynolds (2000).

This is in marked contrast to the Option approach where the child dictates the pace of the interaction: 'The child becomes the teacher – guiding the process…in effect, pointing the way' (Levy 1999, p.2). Here the child is given no guidance as to what an appropriate communication would be.

The Environment

In Proximal Communication, we suggest that a distraction-free environment, such as a soft play area, may enhance the session. This is very different, however, from the Son-Rise principle of having the child in a reduced stimulus therapy room, to remove distractions, for the whole of their waking hours, perhaps over a number of years. Proximal Communication sessions rarely last more than 20 minutes and are only one part of our approach, with other aspects taking place in typical classroom and school settings, so that the child experiences communication in a range of natural environments.

Adult Use of Speech

Another crucial difference between Proximal Communication and the Option approach is in the adult use of speech. In Proximal Communication, as with all of the procedures described in this book, we use a minimal speech approach (see Chapter 3) while the Son-Rise program encourages the use of relatively complex verbal language. A family trainer from the Option Institute gives an example: 'The facilitator might say in a delighted voice: "If you want me to chase you, look into my eyes!"' (Levy 1999, p.5).

The implication is that the child understands the language but may choose not to respond. The facilitator repeats the verbal request several times and, if the child still does not respond, continues the activity anyway, based on the belief that not to do so would in some way disturb the relationship with the child. Our research suggests that the use of this type of language would be more likely to result in children who experienced difficulties understanding speech disengaging from the activity.

A Research Base

We are strongly committed to continuing to develop a sound research foundation to our work. So all of the examples we have used on Proximal Communication here and elsewhere (Whittaker 1996; Whittaker and Reynolds 2000) are based on detailed examination of videotaped evidence and related to other in-depth assessments of the children's abilities. A longitudinal intervention study of communication-enabling approaches, under the heading of Communication Intervention Research in Autism – United Kingdom (CIRA–UK), is also underway. By contrast, the Option Institute indicated that it does not wish to spend time on generating research (Kaufman 1998). Despite this opposition to research, however, Levy (1999) makes some extensive claims for the effectiveness of the Son-Rise approach, including increased language skills; greater eye contact and attention span; improved self-help skills; and 'deeper and stronger human interaction' (p.6) from the child. But he provides no objective evidence for these claims.

Intensive Interaction

Intensive Interaction is a process concerned with pleasurable interaction with children and adults who have severe and profound learning difficulties and limited speech. The process is described in detail in an excellent book by Nind and Hewett (1994), who also undertake very practical workshops with staff and parents. We would strongly recommend their book to anyone interested in using interaction approaches for it covers both the research literature and their approach to practical applications in detail.

SIMILARITIES BETWEEN INTENSIVE INTERACTION AND PROXIMAL COMMUNICATION

Both approaches are designed to engage the child in playful social interactions. Both emphasize a positive view of the child, the importance of building social relationships and the central role of the adult as a key resource in this process of interaction. Both also have a theoretical and practical basis in the literature on early child development which means that the techniques employed are often similar.

DIFFERENCES BETWEEN INTENSIVE INTERACTION AND PROXIMAL COMMUNICATION

Adult Use of Speech

This is a major difference between the two approaches. Nind and Hewett advocate the use of a 'running commentary' where the adult sensitively uses language during the interaction process. This is not a stream of chatter from the adult but involves subtle judgements about timing and appropriateness. They outline their beliefs about this clearly: 'You use spoken language with a person even if you know that your student/client will not understand any of it; the tone of your voice will transmit warmth, participation, and informality' (Nind and Hewett 1994, p.129).

Our data suggests that this 'transmission of warmth, participation and informality' through running commentaries may *not* be helpful for children with autism and minimal speech who were more inclined to disengage from an adult using running commentaries. Indeed, some children appeared distressed by the adult's use of speech in this way. We stressed in Chapter 3 our view that the transmission of empathy is best done non-verbally.

Joining the Child's World

Nind and Hewett (1994) stressed the importance of 'joining the child in his own world' (p.105), including mirroring repetitive behaviour. They see gaining access through carefully matching oneself with the tempo of the child as a long-term process and emphasize that teachers should not expect 'rapid developments' (p.93) with Intensive Interaction. These are subtle points which they make to encourage people to be responsive to children with profound and multiple disabilities, with the expectation that developments will be slow and at the child's pace.

In Proximal Communication we focus on engaging the child quickly, and expecting intentional communication to develop rapidly. We use burst/pause and minimal speech as the key elements in shaping a behaviour that we believe will help the child move on to more conventional systems of communication and we actively try to guide the child away from repetitive behaviours. The significant results which we have documented seem to indicate that Proximal Communication can be effective with many children with autism and minimal speech.

Joint Attention

In Intensive Interaction, adults may introduce a toy or object into the session. As we indicated above we would recommend that Proximal Communication sessions are purely interpersonal, without the use of objects, which seem to distract from the interaction, not enhance it.

Practice Challenges to Implementing Proximal Communication

Having compared other approaches, in this section we will examine some of the professional issues that might arise when considering the introduction of Proximal Communication into the school setting. We are very conscious that although parents may be quite relaxed about using Proximal Communication in their own homes with their own children, professionals may have a number of concerns and reservations.

It may appear developmentally inappropriate and demeaning for the child

This is an important point. However, we believe that our role as adults is to attune ourselves to the child's level of understanding of social communication, not to expect the child to adapt to ours. Proximal Communication builds on the children's strengths and because of their difficulties with communication this means interacting with them at a level of communication which is developmentally lower than many of their other skills, but which is one that they can understand.

Adults may feel it is professionally inappropriate to roll around on the floor imitating vocalizations

Temperamentally, some professionals may feel more inhibited than others in undertaking this work. Effective working groups emphasize individuals' strengths rather than their status, so if one team member was most comfortable in this role then that person might take the lead in this particular activity.

Adults may be worried that the child could get 'over-excited'

Timetabling Proximal Communication sessions for late morning, following more sedentary classroom activities, was found to be very effective in one classroom. It is also important to build time into the Proximal Communication session to give the child (and yourself) time to calm down, cool off and take a rest, particularly when drawing the session to a close. So you may start a session with more rough and tumble play and then go on to a more sedentary activity such as vocal imitation. Always ensure that you and the child are wearing appropriate clothing such as PE kit and tracksuits; it keeps them cool and establishes the right ethos for the activity.

Having said this, we would argue that if the child is getting excited this is not a bad thing. All children need to engage in vigorous physical exercise and this is a positive social context for them to do it. If a child is showing high levels of enjoyment, is establishing a relationship with you and communicating more effectively, then these are very good outcomes.

Staff may feel that others would not see this as educational/therapeutic

When using Proximal Communication, it is vital to provide an explicit written rationale, detailing its educational value in terms of the development of early social and communication abilities. Use of the approach should also be referred to in children's individual education plans.

Safeguards when working with children using approaches which involve physical contact

When classroom staff are using approaches which involve physical contact with children, it is important to ensure that such approaches occur within a framework that is completely open to scrutiny and for which there is an explicit documented rationale. We would recommend both the presence of more than one member of staff and the videotaping of sessions. Videotaping acts both as an open record of such sessions and as a means of monitoring progress over time. Wall-mounted cameras with a wide-angle lens would generally suffice for this. Close collaboration and prior agreement between parents, staff and other involved practitioners is also vital to ensure that everyone understands the nature of the approach and why it is being used. Our personal perspective as professionals, not parents, is that we would not use Proximal Communication with adolescents or with adults, even given the safeguards we have outlined.

Summary Points

- Children in our study communicated most frequently and most spontaneously during Proximal Communication sessions.

- This approach may enable such children to develop a number of early social communication skills.

- The use of a Proximal Communication approach may facilitate the establishment of affective ties and relationships between adults and children with autism.

- Proximal Communication shares some similarities with other therapeutic frameworks but also differs from them in important ways.

5

Prompting for Spontaneous Communication

How we prompt children with communication impairments to communicate significantly affects their ability to become spontaneous communicators (Charlop, Schreibman and Garrison Thibodeau 1985; Halle 1987). The role of prompting in the development of spontaneous communication in children with autism and minimal or no speech, however, is one that has rarely been addressed in the literature.

Key Research Findings

1. Classroom teams had not received training on the role of prompting in the development of spontaneous communication.

2. Video, field note and shadowing data showed that adults very often used a range of verbal prompts, such as questions, to try to encourage children to communicate.

The Effects of Prompting on Spontaneity

Halle (1987) stated that spontaneous communication occurs in response to naturally occurring cues in the environment, rather than in response to prompts to communicate from other people. For example, the emptiness of a cup may prompt one to ask for more water. Halle therefore suggested that we have to help children with severe difficulties in communicating to respond to these naturally occurring prompts in the environment rather than to artificially occurring ones. He asserted that the more adult-directed the prompts we use when we are encouraging children to communicate, the less likely it is that children will learn to communicate spontaneously (see Figure 5.1). This could be particularly true of children with autism because they can easily become prompt dependent. For example, repeated use of verbal prompts can often result in children only being able to respond. Children may learn to sit and wait to be verbally prompted to ask for a drink, so that they become passive rather than active communicators. To exert more control over their environment and to pre-empt frustration borne out of an inability to initiate communication, children need to be able to approach adults and communicate spontaneously about their needs and wants.

Least likely
to lead to
spontaneous communication

Most likely
to lead to
spontaneous communication

Physical guidance	Modelling	Presence of object or situational cue	Presence of listener	Internal feelings
E.g.	E.g.	E.g.	E.g.	E.g.
Physically prompting the child to point	Showing the child how to communicate	Children communicate when they see what they want	Desired item not visible – but adult is nearby	Child feels thirsty and asks for drink

Figure 5.1 Continuum of Cues for Spontaneity
(Adapted from Halle 1987)

Staff Awareness of Current Levels of Prompting

Having understood the role of prompting, the first issue to be considered is to find out how children are currently being prompted to communicate. Given that this might be an area where there has been little previous training for staff, opportunities for discussion and reflection will be necessary. Examples of key questions for staff to reflect on might be:

- When we are trying to encourage David to tell us what he wants (for example, at snack time), what do we do?
- Do we *ask* him what he wants?
- Do we *tell him* to point to what he wants?
- Do we take his hand and *make him point* to what he wants?
- Do we ever wait to see what he will do, by himself, to tell us?
- What is the balance between the uses of these approaches?
- Do we all do the same thing consistently?

We would strongly encourage the supportive use of a range of classroom video clips to enable classroom teams to identify different types of prompts that they are currently using. This will also give them a basis for evaluating future changes.

Why Do Classroom Teams Use the Prompts They Do?

In particular, several authors have discussed the overuse of questions with children having a range of communication impairments. Robson (1989) found that 93 per cent of adult initiations to two children with language difficulties took the form of questions. Wood *et al.* (1986) commented that teachers are 'widely known for their questions', suggesting that questions have traditionally been used in schools as the expected way of gaining appropriate responses from children. We outline below other possible reasons for the extensive use of questions in school settings:

- Staff may believe that children do not have the necessary abilities to initiate communication and therefore they use questions to elicit a response.

- In some situations, staff may feel that they need to get a quicker response from children by using a verbal prompt because other children are becoming impatient.

- Staff may be unaware of other ways of enabling children to communicate more spontaneously.

These are common and understandable reasons for the high use of questions in classrooms.

Why Questions Don't Help

The overuse of questions is unlikely to be helpful for children such as those in our study for a number of reasons. First, due to their severe difficulties in understanding speech, abstract question words such as 'what', 'which' and 'where' are very unlikely to be understood. Second, even though children cannot understand the question words themselves, they may nevertheless come to rely on the verbal cue to communicate – in other words they may become prompt dependent (Charlop and Haymes 1994).

Additionally, the overuse of verbal prompts to communicate requires children to learn only how to make responses and, as we argue throughout this book, the abilities necessary to make responses are not the same as those necessary for initiating a communication. Therefore, children who only have practice in responding may become proficient responders but are unlikely to become proficient spontaneous communicators (see Potter 1996). In the Introduction we examined the human rights issue of being able to initiate communication.

Prompting for Spontaneity

We have seen that children with severe difficulties in communicating are more likely to communicate spontaneously when they are able to respond to naturally occurring environmental cues, rather than to adult generated prompts. The following are examples of naturally occurring environmental cues for communication:

- Alan finds the wrong coat on his coat peg
- David is offered the sort of biscuit he does not like
- Jane cannot do up her zip
- Emma feels thirsty.

How do we enable children to communicate in response to such situational cues rather than adult verbal prompts? First, such an aim is likely to be achieved gradually. Halle (1987) referred to a 'prompt continuum' (see Figure 5.1). The aim should be to move from adult-directed prompts (e.g. physical prompts) to less adult-directed cues (e.g. naturally occurring cues) over time. Halle included the use of questions on his continuum. We have omitted this type of prompt, as children such as those in our study are extremely unlikely to understand many 'wh' question forms such as 'which, where, when, who, what', and therefore these should be avoided.

It may well be necessary to use the most adult-directed form of prompt to begin with, that is a physical prompt, such as moulding a child's hand to form a point. We should aim to reduce the physical prompts as soon as possible, however, by moving on to expecting children to communicate their wants in response to the presence of the things they desire or need. For example, we can gradually reduce the physical prompt and expect the child to point when he sees the desired object in front of him. The intention is that eventually the child will be able to communicate needs and wants in response to internal stimuli, such as feeling hungry, although this is likely to be a longer term aim for many children. Children can easily slip back into previous ways of communicating, for example, a point can become a reach. Then the staff would briefly revert to a physical prompt as a reminder, but always retain the aim of moving to more spontaneous levels of communication.

In Box 5.1 we give an example showing how an adult enabled a child to communicate more spontaneously by using less adult-directed prompts.

Box 5.1

Practice Scenario: A Continuum Approach to Prompting During a Playdough Session

Setting the Scene

- Heather, a teacher, was sitting with David, a child in our study, about to engage in a session with playdough.

- Heather wanted David to choose which tool he wanted to use with the playdough and said, 'Which one do you want, David?' (a verbal question prompt).

Effects on Child Communication

- David responded to the verbal cue by taking one of the tools offered (even though it is very unlikely that he understood the words themselves).

Suggestions for Change

- We suggested that Heather try to move on to the less adult-directed prompt: *'presence of object'* (see Figure 5.1). This means trying to enable David to communicate in response to seeing the object without any verbal prompting from the adult.

- So, instead of asking a question, Heather held up two tools in front of David and said nothing.

Effects of the Change on David's Communication

- Initially, David did not respond, possibly waiting for the adult to ask him what he wanted. Heather pretended to put the tools away in a slow, deliberate way, at which stage he held out his hand towards the one he wanted.

- Here, David was responding to the *presence and possible disappearance of an object* rather than to a verbal prompt.

Benefits of the Changed Approach

- David's communication became more spontaneous as Heather moved from using an adult-directed verbal prompt (a question) to a more environmentally cued one (presence of object). In this way, she is beginning to enable him to focus on what is happening around him and communicate in response to that, rather than focusing on the adult and waiting for her to cue him that it is time to communicate. Such a change in focus will ultimately support David's progression towards becoming an independent and spontaneous communicator.

Enabling Children to Respond to Environmental Cues

Using Long Pauses: Time Delay

What is the most effective way of moving from more adult-directed prompts to more environmentally based ones? The use of pausing (time delay) has been found to be a powerful strategy in prompting communication in children with communication difficulties (Charlop and Trasowech 1991; Leung and Chan 1993; Matson *et al.* 1993). In the example above, the adult working with David introduced a long pause (around 10 seconds) when she held up the tools, instead of asking a question. Introducing time delay into situations where children have specific expectations prompts them:

- actively to focus their attention on the immediate situation instead of waiting passively for the adult to cue them

- to realize that something should be happening

- to become aware that they should try to make it happen

- and finally the pause allows them time to process a communicative behaviour which causes something to happen.

One speech and language therapist in our study told us that she advised parents to count to ten slowly under their breath when trying to use pauses in interactions, to ensure that a long enough delay was introduced. This is very good advice because in everyday interactions a pause of only three to four seconds can seem overlong to fluent communicators. Such a pause is unlikely to be sufficiently long, however, for these children to process the necessary information to produce a communication. In Chapter 4 we examined the use of pauses in Proximal Communication settings.

Contradicting Children's Expectations

In the situation outlined above, the adult pretended to put the tools away, using slow, deliberate actions to give him plenty of time to respond. This was before David had chosen one, thus violating his expectations, which can be a powerful and attention-getting way of enabling children to communicate more spontaneously. Another example of this approach would be where children can be prompted to request their own shoes after PE when they see members of staff pretending to put the children's shoes onto their own feet.

Giving Too Little

Using this strategy, children are prompted to communicate in response to receiving too little of something. Clearly, to use this approach successfully, children must have some expectations of what constitutes an appropriate amount. For example, when presented with jam to spread on toast, only a very small amount could be given. Thus the child is prompted to respond to the environmental cue that there is too little, rather than an adult prompt such as 'do you want more?'.

Interrupting Routines at Critical Points

Behaviour chain interruption has also been documented as a powerful means of teaching children with autism how to initiate communication (Alwell *et al.* 1989; Sigafoos and Littlewood 1999).

This is where children are interrupted in the middle of an ongoing activity to create the need for them to request a continuation of the activity. For example, Sigafoos and Littlewood (1999) reported an increase in the spontaneous requesting of Kurt, a child with autism and minimal speech in his school playground, using this approach. Kurt was frequently stopped in the middle of a play activity in the playground and shown how to request more play (adults said 'say play'). In Halle's terms, this is a 'modelling' type of prompt. Gradually the prompt was faded until Kurt said 'play' without a prompt when interrupted.

Care has to be taken, in such situations, that the interruption does not cause distress. One effective scenario is to use interruption in the making of a familiar item such as a cake, where the teacher pauses at a critical point in the activity and waits for a child to request her to continue.

True Spontaneity: The Ultimate Aim

It is important to emphasize again that all of the strategies described above are only *steps on the path to true spontaneity* where children can initiate a range of communications, for a variety of purposes, with a variety of people, in unstructured situations. In all of the situations described above, adults would almost certainly know what children were going to communicate about. As Watson *et al.* (1989) observed, it is very important that adults should be fully aware that *the ultimate aim of enabling children to become spontaneous communicators is that they can communicate messages which adults are not able to predict.* This is the path that leads to real self-determination for children such as those in our study. However, it is not only what children do which is important. Their empowerment is only achieved when those around them acknowledge and respond to their communications. This is a vital issue and one that is likely to present adults with some dilemmas, which are discussed further in Chapter 7.

Summary Points

- Children with communication impairments are often taught to communicate in response to adult verbal prompts. The overuse of such prompts does not support the development of spontaneous communication.

- Spontaneous communication occurs in response to naturally occurring environmental cues or internally perceived ones.

- Children must therefore be taught to communicate in response to what is happening around them.

- The use of a prompt continuum that enables children to respond to increasingly environmental cues will support children's development as spontaneous communicators.

- The use of long pauses at critical moments during interactions is one particularly effective way of enabling children to respond to environmental cues.

- The ultimate aim is to enable children to communicate new messages to a range of people in their everyday environments.

6

Developing Early Systems of Communication

It has been estimated that as many of 50 per cent of children with autism do not develop speech as a primary means of communication, possibly due to specific motor programming difficulties rather than because of social or cognitive problems (Prizant 1996). Therefore, the need to provide these children with alternative means of communication is vital.

Key Research Findings

1.   The pace and intensity of the introduction of conventional communication systems to children entering school varied between classrooms.

2.   The children in our study used a wide range of conventional and unconventional communicative behaviours to convey their messages. Only two used speech to do so.

3.   The two most frequently used means of communication overall were physical manipulation of another (19 per cent of all spontaneous communications) and re-enactment (12 per cent). Re-enactment is where a child performs part or all of a behaviour sequence associated with a desired outcome. Five children used pointing to communicate. Four of these

children had been taught to do so. Two of them pointed at relatively high rates.

4. These same two children also used multipointing (pointing more than once in sequence) to communicate, both having been taught to do so. They expressed the most complex messages of all of the children in the study.

Developing Conventional Systems of Communication

The fact that children in our study used mostly non-conventional means of communication (such as physical manipulation) to convey their messages is an important issue, which requires some further discussion. Schuler *et al.* (1997) argued that more conventional forms should replace the use of idiosyncratic forms of communication. This may appear somewhat prescriptive. It could be argued that if adults understand children's non-conventional means of communicating, why do more conventional means of communicating need to be taught? The answer is simply that the use of communicative behaviours such as physical manipulation or re-enactment, while possibly effective in the short term, are likely to prove extremely limiting for children in the long or even medium term for a number of reasons.

First, such behaviours enable children to communicate only in very limited ways about the here and now. Second, only adults who know the child well may understand these non-conventional communicative behaviours. Third, such ways of communicating are likely to become less appropriate as children grow older. Finally, all children should be enabled to maximize their learning potential. The intellectual abilities of several children in our study indicated that they were capable of using symbolic systems, which clearly offer access to a much greater range of communicative possibilities. A longitudinal intervention study of some of the children in the present research gives strong support to this view.

Continued reliance on non-conventional ways of communicating may prevent some children from reaching their maximum effectiveness as communicators. How practitioners might begin to introduce more conventional and effective communication systems to young children with autism forms the focus for the remainder of this chapter.

Types of Communication System

Systems of communication can generally be classified as symbolic or non-symbolic. Motoric means of communicating, such as moving someone's hand to a desired object, are non-symbolic; gestural systems such as pointing, while essentially also non-symbolic, are more conventional. Objects of reference are more symbolic where an object is intended to stand for an activity; for example, a ball may represent the idea of going to the ball pool. Pictures, symbols, signs, the written word and speech are wholly symbolic systems, where children have to understand that a picture, sign or word *stands for* an object or a concept. Multipointing has the potential for the child to express complex meanings and grammatical relationships.

Choosing Communication Systems: Key Issues

Watson *et al.* (1989) rightly stated that it is vital to choose a communication system which children can learn to use easily and which enables them to get their messages across in a range of everyday situations. They provided a useful set of guidelines for choosing such systems, stressing the advantages and disadvantages of particular systems as well as providing selection indicators. For example, a pictorial communication system would be appropriate for a child who is interested in pictures and understands that pictures represent concepts. Potential limitations of a pictorial system are that pictures have to be transported between settings, limiting the number of images that can be handled and accessed. Some more abstract concepts, such as verbs and adverbs, complex meanings and grammatical relationships, may also be difficult to illustrate in pictorial form. Symbol systems attempt to overcome these difficulties but may be less accessible to non-users. Printed words are, of course, the most flexible symbolic system of all. Some interesting new results of using printed words with a follow-up group of children from the present study are currently being analysed. Practitioners, therefore, in collaboration with parents, have to weigh potential advantages against disadvantages when choosing communication systems.

Wetherby and Prizant (1992) emphasized that children should be introduced gradually to more than one system of communication so that they have a range of appropriate means of getting messages across. They suggested that one system could be taught as a primary means of communication such as signs, with a different system, like gesture, taught to help children to repair communicative breakdowns. Decisions about choosing a communication system should also be reviewed at regular intervals. As children's capabilities change, other systems of communication may be considered. For example, children who are taught to point may go on to use more complex forms of communication, such as signs, picture symbols, multipointing or the written word.

Early Intervention

The earlier children are introduced to more formal communication systems, the better. Early intervention is accepted as of critical importance in the education of children with autism, with children appearing to benefit most between the ages of 2 and 4 years (Rogers 1996). Rogers reported that the same interventions seemed far less effective with older children. This being the case, it seems important to begin the process of teaching communication systems as quickly as possible. In one of our study classrooms, children were successfully taught to point within a few weeks, using an intensive teaching programme on entering a reception class.

Pointing as an Early Communication System

The occurrence of pointing in infants is seen as important in the development of language use and is therefore considered a vital element in their communicative competence (Foster 1990). There is general agreement that children start to use pointing to communicate early in their second year (Bates *et al.* 1979; Cox 1991) and that pointing can be separated into two main categories according to the purpose it serves. Proto-imperative pointing is where children point to tell adults that they want something. Proto-declarative pointing is where children point to show something to an adult. Evidence suggests that infants use both these types of pointing at about the same time (Hobson 1993). By contrast, it is known that the development of pointing in children with autism does not follow this pattern (Ricks and Wing 1975; Sigman *et al.* 1986). Research has shown that some children with autism may point to ask for something, but that they rarely point to show things to others (Baron-Cohen 1989; Curcio 1978).

The need to teach young children with autism to point as a developmentally appropriate means of communicating their needs and wants has been stressed for some time (Christie and Newson 1998; Christie *et al.* 1992; Christie and Wimpory 1986). The teaching of pointing to children with autism as an early means of communication has been reported to have several advantages:

- It requires minimal symbolic understanding so will be developmentally appropriate for most children.

- It gives the child immediate access to a wide range of communicative possibilities.

- The pointing behaviour is easily shaped.

- There will be many opportunities to practise it throughout the day.

Box 6.1 details how children in one classroom were taught to point initially.

Box 6.1

Practice Scenario: Teaching Peter to Point in a 1:1 Setting

- Heather, the teacher, sat across the table from Peter.

- Heather used equipment or materials known to be motivating for Peter and well within his capabilities – a car run where a small car rolls down a number of zigzagging ramps.

- Heather first gained Peter's attention by saying his name clearly.

- She then held up the car and immediately shaped his index finger on his dominant hand to form a point. She then physically prompted him to touch the car with this finger. As soon as Peter's finger had touched the car, she put the car at the top of the ramp and let it go for him to watch.

- Heather used a minimal speech approach, saying nothing until the car was let go on the ramp when she said 'Go!' thus ensuring that the child was exposed only to the most relevant vocabulary in the situation (see Chapter 3).

- When the car reached the bottom, Heather quickly scooped it up and repeated the process.

- Over a number of sessions, she reduced the physical prompts until Peter was pointing independently. As discussed throughout this book, reducing communicative prompts as soon as possible helps to promote spontaneous communication.

- The activity chosen by this teacher constituted an ideal joint action routine for the child in question, since it was short, repetitive and motivating to him, with clearly defined roles for both the adult and the child.

- The shortness of the routine is very important since the activity can be repeated frequently to ensure that the child has many opportunities to learn and practise the skills of pointing in a short space of time.

- This frequency of practice seems important for children to learn the skill. We observed that when children had only four or five opportunities to learn to point during the school day, they did not learn to point so rapidly or spontaneously.

- Children can quickly be introduced to choice making in these individual teaching sessions, where the adult may hold up two items or activities for children to choose from.

Generalizing Pointing Skills to Engineered Situations

We observed that Heather also engineered opportunities during many everyday situations throughout the school day for Peter to practise his newly acquired skills. A list of such opportunities is shown in Table 6.1.

Table 6.1 Pointing opportunities during the school day	
Activity	**Pointing Opportunity**
PE	Pointing to clothes to put on
Snack	Pointing to food items, choose between two
Playtime	Pointing to child's own coat
Painting	Pointing to colour of paint, type of tool (brush, sponge)
Lotto	Pointing to counters
Bubbles	Pointing to pot
Leaving the classroom	Pointing to door

Multipointing

Once children in Heather's class had begun to point fluently and spontaneously, they were taught to multipoint to enable them to communicate more complex messages. Multipointing is the use of sequences of points, to convey a single complex message, described by Potter and Whittaker (1997). This approach enables children to convey more complex messages without needing to know the necessary individual signs, words or symbols. Through multi-pointing, children were taught to convey a range of meanings, including action, location, possession and agent. Examples of such meanings are shown in Table 6.2.

Table 6.2 Multipointing to convey a range of meanings			
Meaning	**Definition**	**Example of Message**	**Multipointing**
Action	Asking for something to be done	Child wants adult to do up a button	Point to adult and button
Location	Asking to go somewhere or asking for something to be moved somewhere	Child wants adult to put a picture in his bag	Point to picture and bag
Agent	Indicating who should do something	Child or adult to blow bubbles	Point to self (child) and bubbles. Point to adult and bubbles
Possession	To whom something belongs	Child wants to play with own toy	Point to toy and self

In Box 6.2 we describe how Heather taught Emma to multipoint by using a matching activity. The meaning being taught was location.

Box 6.2

Teaching Emma to Multipoint in an Intensive 1:1 Setting

- Heather sat next to Emma.

- There were two clear plastic boxes on the table in front of them. One picture was put in one box and a different picture in the other. Emma was already able to match pictures easily and could point spontaneously.

- Heather held up a picture identical to one of those in a box and physically prompted Emma to point, first to the picture she was holding and then to the matching picture in the box. Heather then put the picture into the box and held up another.

- Within a single session this sequence was repeated quickly several times.

- Gradually the prompts were faded so that Emma began to multipoint spontaneously.

Again, it is important to emphasize the importance of working with materials that children enjoy using and which are well within their capabilities so that they can focus on the new skill of multipointing. Other types of equipment could be used to teach children to express the same meaning, for example, moving bricks to the top of a brick tower or moving puzzle pieces to the correct place in the jigsaw.

Generalizing Multipointing Skills to Engineered Situations

Once Emma could multipoint in this highly structured individual session, Heather created numerous opportunities throughout the school day for her to practise these skills:

- At drinks time, Emma was prompted to point first to the biscuit tin and then to her own plate, to convey the message *put a biscuit on my plate.*

- During structured painting sessions, she was prompted to indicate to staff, using multipointing, where on her paper to put extra paint. Here the major aim was *communication*. Free painting took place at other times.

Once more, prompts were gradually faded so that Emma was multipointing spontaneously in these less structured and more distracting situations.

Spontaneous Use of Multipointing

The real aim is for the children to be able to use their skills to convey new and spontaneous messages. For example, in an observed soft-play session, Emma pointed first to an adult's hand and then to her own legs, indicating that she wanted the teacher to pick her up. During lunchtime, Emma used her multipointing skills to convey a complex message concerning location. By using a sequence of points, she was spontaneously able to ask an adult to put some crisps back into her lunch box and the chocolate biscuit on to her plate in the course of a single communication. She achieved this by pointing first to the crisps, then to the lunchbox and then to the biscuit and finally to her plate.

Emma did not use speech to communicate at this time and understood very little spoken language. This scenario raises some very interesting theoretical questions. For example, is multipointing tapping into mental representational structures that allow her to communicate complex messages in the absence of conventional language? This aspect of multipointing warrants further detailed research.

Grammatical Aspects of Multipointing

One aspect of our videotaped multipointing data that we are exploring further is the syntax of particular communications. Our impression is that children who multipointed rarely made errors of syntax when doing so. For example, in the scene described above, Emma pointed *first* to the crisps and then to the lunchbox – and not the other way around. Heather related an interesting incident where this child did make a syntactical error when multipointing. Emma was trying to communicate the message *you put the juice into my cup* – by pointing to Heather, then the juice and then the cup. Instead of pointing in this sequence, Emma pointed first to Heather, then to the cup and then to the juice. Heather immediately complied by putting the cup into the jug of juice since this is what Emma had communicated. Seeing this, Emma began to laugh and once the cup was taken out of the juice, Emma produced the correct sequence, thus indicating her awareness of the necessary ordering of points in the message.

Multipointing in Academic and Assessment Tasks

An important use of multipointing is in the assessment and teaching of academic skills. In one of our study classrooms, multipointing was used in the context of a range of increasingly complex cognitive tasks with some of the children. Examples were: helping children simply to indicate where a puzzle piece should go; using multipointing in picture and sound lotto games; supporting their understanding of mathematical tasks, such as matching numerals to two-dimensional groups of objects; and in word recognition tasks. The use of multipointing by the teacher in these situations seemed to help children to understand more easily what was to be done. It also enabled children to indicate their own understanding of these tasks by pointing in sequence themselves. Multipointing can also give children access to formal non-verbal IQ tests, denied to those without these communication skills.

A Possible Additional Function of Multipointing

We observed another possible function of multipointing in one of our study classrooms. Two children who used sequences of points to communicate were observed to multipoint to themselves, that is, to use sequences of points in situations where they were working independently, without an adult nearby. For example, when independently matching colour cards, Aaron was seen to point first to one card and then to the matching one. One explanation is that Aaron was simply repeating a sequence that he had been taught to use in individual sessions with his teacher. Another more intriguing possibility, but one that is difficult to demonstrate, is that this multipointing to self could be construed as a non-verbal equivalent to externalizing 'inner speech' linked to thought processes, which is frequently observed in young children. This is an issue that we hope to explore further in future research.

Using Symbols

In another classroom, we observed children learning to use symbols to make requests. A number of small cardboard squares, representing various activities, were attached by Velcro to a long piece of card at child height. Adults would take the child to the strip and offer a symbol to the child (e.g. shiny paper card to indicate sound and light room). Children could accept or refuse the card. We observed one child begin to make spontaneous requests by taking the cards off the strip himself and giving them to adults only a few weeks after joining the class.

Learning to Use Communication Systems: Key Points

In another classroom, staff communicated with children using a combination of signs, symbols and speech, which they termed a 'total communication' approach. During a feedback session at this school, the use of signing with non-verbal children with autism was discussed. It emerged that none of the children with whom signing was being used had spontaneously begun to use signs to communicate themselves. This discussion highlighted two key issues which merit further exploration. The first is that in order for children to be able to understand signing, they must be capable of understanding that a sign, symbol or word *stands for* something else. If children are not at this intellectual level, then signing will be too complex for them. If children do have the capacity for using a symbolic means of communication, then signing may be easier for them to understand than speech, since signs exist in visual space and can be maintained over time, allowing the children more time to process the information. There is a great difference, however, between children being able to understand signs and being able to use them.

Specific fine motor skills are necessary to produce signs that are intelligible to others and this may be difficult for some children. Children also have to be motivated to use specific signs for specific purposes. We believe that children at the early stages of communicating may learn the power of communication more successfully using physically simpler communication systems to begin with, such as pointing and multipointing. Once they become proficient, intentional communicators, then more symbolic systems of communication may be introduced more successfully. In this way, the demands of each stage of learning to communicate are reduced. To expect children to learn how to communicate intentionally at the same time as learning to do so symbolically may well create unnecessary obstacles to successful communication for some of them.

The actual means by which messages are produced (speech or signing, for example) is only one aspect of the abilities which children with autism need to initiate communication. The use of signs or symbols in the classroom by staff will not usually result, on its own, in children being able to use these communication systems themselves. In the majority of cases, these children will need to be specifically taught to use chosen communication systems, first in intensive one-to-one teaching situations and later in semi-structured engineered settings.

Children's use of whatever communication system is being taught will improve significantly if many opportunities to practise the use of these systems are provided in a wide range of contexts. We observed high levels of proficiency in the use of multipointing in one classroom where very many communication opportunities were provided for the children to practise these skills throughout the school day.

Diversifying Communication Systems Over Time

As discussed above, individual educational programmes need to account for children's changing needs and capabilities in terms of communication systems. For example, children in one of our study classrooms were taught first to point, then, depending on the rate of learning, they were taught to multipoint. Later, some of these children were introduced to word recognition tasks, as it became apparent that their visual perception and symbolic abilities were sufficiently well developed to support such systems. In future it is hoped that they will be able to use printed words to communicate, as well as multipointing. There will be some situations where pointing will be more effective than written words. For example, during Proximal Communication sessions, children may use multipointing to indicate which particular social routine they want the adult to engage in: for example, child points to adult and then to feet to indicate they want the feet tickling game. In using an individual or class timetable words or pictures may be more appropriate.

Whatever the communication system, it is essential that children are given every opportunity to become fluent in its use as quickly as possible.

Summary Points

- For children who do not use speech as their primary means of communication, it is essential to introduce them, as quickly as possible, to alternative conventional means of getting their messages across.

- Intensive individual teaching appears to be the most effective way of enabling children to learn how to use the chosen system.

- Pointing and multipointing seem to be particularly useful early systems of communication.

- Children's communication systems require regular review as their communicative and cognitive abilities develop.

- Where possible, it is advisable to provide children with more than one communication system.

7

Creating Communication-rich Environments

Children with communication difficulties require very frequent opportunities to practise their communication skills (Rowland 1990; Sigafoos *et al.* 1994a; Wall and Dattilio 1995). In this chapter we will explore approaches we found to be effective in ensuring that children have access to many and varied communication opportunities throughout the day, in the whole range of school contexts.

Key Research Findings

1. Those children who were provided with the most opportunities to communicate spontaneously communicated most.

2. Opportunities to communicate were created by adults more frequently in some situations and classrooms than in others.

3. Most communication opportunities offered in classroom-based situations were for children to make requests for an object – either an activity or an item of food.

4. Proximal Communication sessions provided particularly high rates of opportunities for communication.

5. Few opportunities for children to communicate directly with each other were engineered.

6. Few opportunities for children to learn how to protest or get attention were created.

The Importance of Creating Opportunities for Communication

Research has shown that children with communication difficulties often receive insufficient opportunities to practise their communication skills. For example, deaf-blind children were offered few such opportunities within their classroom environments over a one-year period (Rowland 1990). Sigafoos *et al.* (1994b) found that children with communication impairments in special education classrooms were offered only the same number of opportunities to communicate as typically developing children in day care centres, when clearly they required many more.

Svavarsdottir (1992) found that the communication opportunities offered to children with autism being educated in specialist TEACCH classrooms in North Carolina were generally limited to transition periods when children moved from one activity to another. She also observed that the type of communicative opportunity offered at these times was repetitive, allowing pupils to practise only the same communication abilities each day. This is surprising, given that TEACCH has emphasized spontaneous communication as a key element of their approach (Watson *et al.* 1989).

Peck (1989) noted that many aspects of the communication which occurs between adult and child are affected by the nature of the situation in which the communication is taking place. In instructional situations, for example, he maintained that there are likely to be fewer opportunities for children to initiate communication because these sessions tend to be mainly adult directed. Classrooms in which children are seen as passive recipients of knowledge imparted by the teacher are much less likely to enhance spontaneous communication than environments where children are encouraged to be active learners.

The need to provide children with functionally relevant communication opportunities has also been discussed. Sigafoos and York

(1991) suggested that it is vital to provide students with opportunities to learn those communication skills that are most useful in their everyday environments.

Difficulties can arise in school situations because classrooms are essentially artificially created communication environments. Wood *et al.* (1986) highlighted this fact:

> Schools were never designed to foster the intimate, two-way, reciprocal and contingent interactions that seem best suited to the development of communication between adults and children. Indeed they are more likely to achieve the opposite state of affairs by demanding that children 'pay attention' and pursue goals established by adults. (Wood *et al.* 1986, p.47)

The challenge for practitioners, therefore, is to create as many meaningful opportunities as possible for communication within the context of everyday school activities.

Dimensions of Communication Opportunities

Our research identified a number of different dimensions relating to communication opportunities that need to be taken into account when planning a communication-enabling environment.

Frequency and Clustering of Communicative Opportunity

The frequency of communication opportunities would appear to have at least two dimensions. The first relates to the overall number of such opportunities created per day. In order to enable children with significant communication impairments to develop their skills, research suggests that such opportunities should be offered frequently (Rowland and Schweigert 1993). Findings from our own research would also indicate that the grouping of many opportunities together within a short space of time is also important for maximum learning to occur. Proximal Communication sessions in some classrooms provided several high quality communicative opportunities per minute and within such sessions children began to communicate more intentionally, spontaneously and frequently. Frequent communication opportunities were created in other types of individual session. For example, in one such session, a teacher created 18 opportunities for a child to ask her to blow bubbles over a three-minute period, by using a time delay approach. After she blew the bubbles, she deliberately waited, saying nothing, until the child communicated that he wanted her to blow more of them.

Type of Communicative Opportunity

In order to communicate for a variety of purposes, children will need to have access to a range of communicative opportunities which allow them to practise these skills. For example, during snack sessions the most usual kind of communication opportunities created were requests for food or drink. Children could, however, be taught to communicate for other purposes during these sessions.

At an appropriate stage in their communication development, children could be offered non-preferred items to allow them to practice communicating refusals during snack time.

Adults could create opportunities for children to practise getting attention by deliberately looking away from the table. Another adult should be on hand here to prompt a 'get attention' behaviour, for example, by physically prompting the child to tap the adult's arm. The teaching of a 'get attention' signal will generally be taught later in the communication development of children with autism and minimal or no speech, after they have learnt to make requests in a range of settings for different purposes and with different people Watson et al. (1989).

Wetherby and Prizant (1992) stressed the difference between children communicating to ask people to do something *functional* for them (e.g. do up a zip) and children asking people to do something for a more *social* purpose (e.g. tickle them). It is important to be aware of these differences and to give children opportunities to practise communicating both types of request.

Characteristics of High Quality Communication Opportunities

The creation of high quality opportunities for communication is a complex and skilful endeavour, during which a number of factors have to be considered by the adult facilitator.

Motivation

It is vital that children are sufficiently motivated by aspects of the situation to want to communicate. Children such as those in our study experience complex difficulties in communicating with others and such problems will be greatly compounded by expecting them to communicate in situations that they actively dislike, even after becoming familiar with them. It is, therefore, very important for staff to identify as wide a range of activities as possible in which children show obvious enjoyment.

Social activities involving Proximal Communication can be highly motivating for many children. We saw in Chapter 4 that although many children may enjoy the rough and tumble aspects of these sessions, others may prefer quieter games during which there is vocal imitation of the child by the adult. An example of the communication motivators of one child in our study is given in Box 7.1.

Box 7.1

Emma's Communication Motivators

- Proximal Communication sessions
- Snack sessions
- Sound Lotto
- Matching tasks
- Sand play
- Craft sessions
- Lego construction

It is important for children to have regular access to favourite activities in order to ensure optimum conditions for communication development.

Means of Communication

Children must have appropriate communication systems for conveying relevant messages in any given situation. For example, during a pause in a tickling game they must have some way of communicating 'more' – for example, by looking at the adult, by pointing to the adult or by making a sign for tickling. When setting up an opportunity for communication, adults must either know that children have such behaviour within their communication repertoire or must be ready to prompt them to produce such behaviour.

Repetition

Our research suggested that at least some communication opportunities during the day should be presented repeatedly within a short space of time, as suggested above. Such repetition appears to support much more rapid learning than when opportunities are spaced out throughout the day. There are many appropriate situations for such repetition: for example, during Proximal Communication sessions; snack time; playdough; painting; looking at books; constructional activities.

Prompting for Spontaneous Communication

As discussed in Chapter 5, how adults prompt children to communicate is critical to the development of spontaneous communication. The aim should always be to try to enable children to communicate in response to environmental cues rather than to adult prompts. In practice, this means that adults need to move away from using non-naturally occurring stimuli, such as adult physical and verbal prompts, and towards children responding to classroom cues such as the sight of a bottle of juice or a toy out of reach.

Proximity

With children at the early stages of communication, it is important to be close to the child and level with his/her eye gaze or below it, depending on the activity. Try to avoid being in the dominant position of looking down at the child.

Clarity

All aspects of the communication opportunity need to be extremely clear to the child. Distractions should be minimized. For example, in snack sessions, the table should be clear so that children can easily focus on snacks offered to them by classroom staff. Children must know from the context what there is to communicate about and when it is their turn to communicate. Adults should give children explicit cues in their body language that it is their turn to do something: for example, by using facial expressions that convey expectancy (large eyes, raised eyebrows). Speech, of course, should be kept to a minimum.

Programme Related Communicative Opportunities

Types of communication opportunity being offered should relate to the children's current individual programme goals. For example, children may be learning to communicate about where things should go (location) by multipointing. Classroom teams may then create opportunities for this type of message to be expressed in a variety of contexts. At snack time, children could be expected to point first to the juice jug and then to their cup, for example. When playing with bricks, adults could withhold some bricks until children communicate where to put them by pointing first to the brick and then to a tower. Staff should be expecting children to convey novel messages during later stages of teaching.

The remainder of this chapter is concerned with enabling classroom staff to rethink everyday school activities in terms of how to use them to create as many meaningful opportunities for communication as possible.

Identifying Communication Opportunities in Everyday Situations

Practitioners need to become aware of the types of communication opportunities that are currently being offered to children. Often, given the many and varied pressures of a school day, it may be difficult to identify the frequency and nature of opportunities which are currently being provided. Yet before embarking on a process of change it is necessary to have an accurate record of the existing situation. Videotape, although time consuming to analyse, can provide extensive data. Relevant information can also be logged on a simple chart. An example of a possible format for such observations is provided in Table 7.1, where one adult is recording the number of communication opportunities offered to one particular child by other

Table 7.1 Possible format for the observation of communication opportunities

Date: 2.3.00 Child: Emma Time of observation: 10.45–11.45

Communication Opportunity Offered	Number	Total
Giving choice of activity, equipment, and food.	IIII	4
Stopping part-way through an activity or social interaction to elicit request to continue.	II	2
Giving small portions to elicit request for more.	0	0
Making items inaccessible to elicit request.	II	2
Giving children materials that they will need help with, to elicit asking for help.	I	1
Contradicting children's expectations to elicit request or comment.	0	0
Giving children known non-preferred items to elicit protest.	0	0
Actively withdrawing attention to elicit 'get attention' request.	0	0
Total		9

members of staff over a one hour period. Notice that it is only what the adult does that is recorded here.

In Table 7.1, adults only engineered opportunities for Emma to make requests during the one-hour observation. This may be in keeping with her individual education plan where the goal is for her to make requests for objects and requests for help. Alternatively, if a goal is for her to seek adult attention when she needs it, then perhaps insufficient opportunities are being created.

A Continuum Approach to Prompting

Once a communication opportunity has been created, it is important to adopt a continuum approach to prompting, with the focus on *responding to environmental cues* rather than adult spoken prompts. For example:

- Children should be prompted to ask the teacher to open the door by the fact that the door remains closed, *not by a spoken prompt.*

- Children can be prompted to ask for more juice by empty cups, *not by a spoken prompt to ask.*

- Children may be prompted to indicate 'again' by the pause in the rhyme, *not by a spoken prompt to request more.*

There are a number of different types of opportunity for communication which children could be offered. If children are only offered opportunities to ask for objects (snacks or toys), it is unlikely that they will spontaneously learn how to ask for help, to protest or to get attention, yet these are all important abilities. Table 7.2 highlights questions that may help staff to identify such opportunities.

Table 7.2 Identifying Communication Opportunities	
Reflective Questions	Possible Communication Opportunities
Are there parts of this activity that children cannot do by themselves?	There may be an opportunity for children to ask for help.
Are there aspects of this activity that may allow for preferences to be expressed?	There may be opportunities for children to make choices.
Is the time span for this activity fixed or could children decide when to finish?	There may be opportunities for children to ask to stop or continue.
Could children decide where to sit for this activity?	There may be opportunities for children to ask to sit in a particular place.
Must children complete all aspects of this activity?	Children could choose to decline various aspects of the activity.

These important questions can be raised during staff training days and/or during discussions on individual education programmes. The ultimate aim is for staff to internalize these reflective ways of working so that they can quickly maximize communication opportunities in any given situation.

Communication Opportunities Throughout the Day

In Table 7.3 we have outlined examples of communication opportunities that we saw engineered in the context of the study classrooms. By providing children with such opportunities to communicate their needs and wants, classroom teams shift the focus away from purely adult-directed environments towards more child-led ones. Such opportunities enable children to learn how to become more self-determined, and to exert more control over their immediate environment. Achieving an appropriate balance between adult-led and child-led scenarios forms an important goal in the area of enabling

these children to progress towards optimum levels of personal
autonomy.

Table 7.3 Examples of communication opportunities in the classroom		
Time	**Session/Activity**	**Communication Opportunities Offered**
9.00 am	Choice of activity while other children are arriving	Choice – request for object/equipment Request to continue or reject continued use of equipment
9.30 – 10.30 am	Group divided – children rotate between independent work, individual work and Proximal Communication sessions	
	Independent work TEACCH boxes – some necessary equipment deliberately missing	Request missing equipment
	Individual work Learning new task	Choice – request order of tasks Choice – request colour of pencil
	Proximal Communication session	Request action (social) Request continuation of social routine Reject continuation of social routine
10.30 am	Getting ready for playtime	Request for action (functional) (putting coat on) Request for action (functional) (adult to open door)
10.30 – 10.45 am	Playtime	Request for action (social) – adult plays chase or ball game

10.45 – 11.00 am	Drinks	Request for object (drink) Reject one drink in favour of another Request more (drink) Request food Reject food
11.00 – 11.40 am	Ball pool	Request for social routine (e.g. chasing) Request for continuation of social routine Reject social routine Choice – request for different social routine
11.45 – 12.00	Book session	Choice – request book Request location – where to sit – table or rug
12.00 pm	Lunchtime	Request social routine – which child to hold hands with going to the dining room Request food/drink Request more food Reject food/drink
12.30 – 1.00 pm	Playtime	Request for social game (chase/ball game etc.)
1.10 – 1.40 pm	Painting session	Choice – request item (colour of apron) Choice – request item (colour of paper) Choice – request item (large/small paintbrush; sponge etc.) Choice – request item (colour of paint) Reject activity (choose to stop painting)

1.45 – 2.15 pm Group divided	Computer session	Request action – adult to switch computer on Choice – request activity – choose particular programme Reject activity – choose to finish programme Choice – request activity – choose a different programme
	Walk to local shop	Request action (functional) – help to put coat on Request action – adult to open door Request action (social) – who to walk with
2.30 – 2.45 pm	Multisensory room	Request action – adult to switch on particular pieces of equipment Request action – adult to operate equipment Request action (social) – rhyme, e.g. 'Wind the Bobbin Up', etc.
2.45 – 3.00 pm	Drinks	Request for object (drink) Reject drink Request more (drink) Request food Reject food
3.05 pm	Home time	Request action (functional) – put coat on

The examples in Table 7.3 are intended to represent only possible communication opportunities that may occur in everyday sessions. The list is certainly not exhaustive and it is probable that once practitioners are alerted to the notion of communication opportunities, they will be able to identify more of them across a range of contexts. It is likely to be neither appropriate nor practicable to offer every child every opportunity. For example, staff may wish to focus exclusively on enabling one child to make requests for social routines for a specified period of time. It may be a priority for another child to learn how to express protests in an appropriate manner.

It will almost certainly be necessary to familiarize many children with the normal running of a particular activity before introducing choice factors. For example, children will need to experience what it is like to use a sponge as opposed to a paintbrush before they can be expected to make a choice about which they would prefer to use in a craft session.

Different Types of Communication Opportunity

Asking for Help

Children with autism can become extremely frustrated and distressed if they do not know how to ask for help. Unfortunately, they may resort to challenging behaviours to achieve certain goals in the absence of appropriate communicative abilities. Therefore, it is vital to provide many opportunities for these children to learn how to ask for help in a wide range of situations.

There are many opportunities throughout the school day where children will need help. Often, in the busy setting of a classroom, however, these opportunities may be overlooked or the need to ask for help can be pre-empted by adults for a number of reasons. Caring classroom teams are expert in knowing what children's needs are likely to be in a wide range of everyday school situations and may become adept at meeting them before the children themselves have realized that they have these wants. This sometimes over-efficient meeting of needs may be grounded in adult concerns that children may become distressed if needs are not immediately met.

This is a valid concern and the relevant teaching point is that when adults decide to let children become aware that they cannot do something, they must be on hand to model an 'asking for help' communication as soon as children show signs of uncertainty, and before they show any agitation. At first, children may be physically prompted completely through the communication behaviour after which the adult immediately complies with the request. Only when children become comfortable with this new approach and know how to ask for help should adults begin to wait to see if they will ask more spontaneously. Such a process is more empowering for children because it gives them the opportunity to think about what is happening in their environment and then to communicate about it.

THE TEACHING PROCESS

There are a few points to be made relating to when and how children should be encouraged to learn to ask for help. First, there are several stages in this process, which may have to be taught separately. In order to ask for help, children have to be able to do the following:

- realize that they need help;
- realize that other people can supply this help;
- know how to attract such a person's attention;
- know what the right message is;
- have a communication system that enables them to get the message across (e.g. pointing, signing, pictures).

Second, there is obviously a balance to be struck between using self-help situations, for example, as opportunities for communication and using them to develop independence skills. Staff will be guided by their own judgement on these matters. Young children are likely to need help with some aspects of dressing for quite some time, though this situation represents an extremely powerful communicative opportunity.

EXAMPLES

The following are suggestions for engineering opportunities for children to ask for help. In each situation, adults should try to enable children to communicate in response to the environmental cues as opposed to verbal requests to communicate (see Chapter 5):

- Wait until children realize that they cannot undo their seatbelt at the end of a minibus trip and then prompt a communication which the child could use to ask for help, for example, by physically prompting them to point to the adult and then to the seatbelt.

- Put favourite toys on transparent shelves out of reach.

- Keep drinks and snack food on show but out of reach at snack time.

- Become aware of the communication opportunities in self-help areas such as dressing, undressing, getting dry after swimming.

- Give children equipment with lids and tops still in place, so that they will either have to take them off themselves or realize that they cannot do it when they can be taught to request help.

- Do not automatically give out expected equipment for activity sessions, e.g. water-play equipment; sand-play equipment. Instead, allow children time to perceive that there are no toys in the sand or water, and then to realize that they want some and finally to communicate about this wish.

Opportunities to Protest

During the course of our research, we did not observe many communication opportunities deliberately engineered to elicit protests. This may well be because many children were relatively new to full-time education and therefore other communication goals may have been more appropriate in these early stages.

Understandably, children's rejections are often viewed as negative behaviours indicating their reluctance to participate in certain activities. For children with significant communication difficulties, however, it seems important to teach them how to protest appropriately to pre-empt the development of less desirable behaviours to fulfil this function. More appropriate protesting behaviours, for example, might be pushing away an adult's hand or signing 'no'.

The right to express a protest is fundamental to our status as self-determined individuals and most people will make use of this right in a range of situations several times a day. Children with and without impairments also have this right, although to exercise it may present us, as adults, with a number of dilemmas, some of which are discussed below.

DILEMMAS IN TEACHING CHILDREN TO PROTEST

First, staff will need to judge when to offer children the opportunity to protest. There will be occasions when practitioners may judge it best to override protests in the short term in order to encourage children to participate for at least a short while before leaving an activity. Teachers in our study reported that often children actively resisted new activities to begin with, but later could find them enjoyable.

Similarly, when young children with autism first attend educational settings, there may be an adjustment period when they resist participation in many activities. Staff will usually choose to introduce children to a range of activities gradually for short periods of time, after which extended protests will often diminish.

OPPORTUNITIES TO TEACH BETTER WAYS OF PROTESTING

Once children have gained enough experience of the whole range of school activities, it may be appropriate to teach them how to register protest, thereby affording them greater control over their environment and pre-empting the development of other less appropriate behaviours to express refusal.

QUESTIONS TO ASK WHEN CONSIDERING A PROTEST

Below are a number of questions, which may help practitioners to make decisions about possible responses to children's protests.

- Is this a reasonable protest, in the circumstances?
- Are there valid reasons why children may not want to participate in this activity today (illness, tiredness, the task is too easy/too difficult/too long/over-familiar)?
- Are we contributing to the problem by using too much speech or by sitting children too close together?

- Is the pace of this activity too quick or too slow for particular children?

- Do children really need to do this now? Could they do it later, instead?

- Could they do less of it?

Adults could engineer situations in which to teach children to communicate 'no'. For example, at snack time, children could be offered a snack that they are known not to favour. If children do begin to display rejecting behaviours (facial grimace or vocalizations), adults should quickly demonstrate or physically prompt the more appropriate signal chosen for that child to indicate 'no'. This could be prompting the child to push the item way or to sign 'no'. Having done this, the adult should quickly remove the item and then offer items that the child is known to like.

If it is thought important for the child to engage in particular activities, protests may be accepted for the time being on the understanding that a small part of the task will be completed before the end of the session. The use of visual cues and routines, such as the 'work then play' structured teaching approaches, can be useful in encouraging children to participate in non-preferred activities (Schopler 1995). It is important for staff to reflect upon how much time children are being required to spend engaging in non-preferred as opposed to preferred activities. Maintaining an appropriate balance in this area is vital to ensure high levels of child motivation.

IDENTIFYING SITUATIONS IN WHICH CHILDREN ARE GIVEN THE REAL OPPORTUNITY TO PROTEST

There are a number of situations in which children could legitimately be given the opportunity to protest or refuse during the school day. For example:

- Children may choose to reject a particular activity in an unstructured play session.

- There may be occasions when children could choose the time at which they will disengage from an activity.

- Children could refuse extra helpings, or food they did not like, at lunchtime.

Opportunities to Communicate Through Problem Solving

Another type of valuable communicative opportunity is the use of naturally occurring situations for children to think critically about what is happening in their environment and communicate about it. Enabling children with autism to become effective problem solvers is recognized as an important teaching goal (Jordan and Powell 1995) since it leads to greater self-determination (Wehemeyer 1996).

An early problem-solving scenario might be to encourage children to make decisions on what is necessary to carry on with an activity and then communicate them. To make such decisions, children first need to be familiar with the equipment and process necessary to complete a particular activity. It may be necessary to repeat the activity several times before the adult can begin to plan for problem-solving practice within that process.

For example, if the activity were making a mousse, children could be offered both a spoon and a cup when the mixing stage is reached. They are thus encouraged to consider which piece of equipment is necessary to achieve that particular task and to communicate their decision through multipointing, for example (by pointing first to the spoon and then to the mixture).

There are numerous occasions during the day when children can be encouraged to reflect on aspects of their environment and communicate about them. For example, when going out to play, two coats could be offered so that children have to identify which is their own. When getting dressed after PE, adults could hold up two items of clothing (vest and jumper, for example) to encourage the children to consider which item needs to be put on first.

The aim of such practice is to enable children to begin to think more flexibly about what is happening in their environment and, most importantly, to help them make decisions about what should happen in particular situations and to learn how to communicate those decisions. Adults will need to judge how many such opportunities to offer children as well as when to offer them. If children are tired, appear unwell or are obviously anxious about other things, problem solving may not be an ideal teaching focus that day.

Another important issue is that by providing frequent opportunities for children to reflect on their environment, it is likely that they will become more engaged in what is happening around them. This was certainly the case for the children in our study. When activities proceed too smoothly due to adults providing the right equipment or cues at the right moment, children with autism can easily become passive recipients rather than active learners. Although we agree that children with autism certainly need predictability and structure, it is vital that once children understand their environment and have clear expectations about it, adults introduce cognitive and communicative challenges to maintain motivation and enhance participation.

Opportunities to Communicate Through Making Choices

Brown and Cohen (1996) have charted the change in curricular focus for children with severe impairments, from a time when independence skills referred only to self-help tasks, to a more recent emphasis on independence through personal empowerment.

This need for people with impairments to achieve self-determination is now the focus of much current thinking in the field of special education (Coupe O'Cane and Smith 1994; Wall and Dattilio 1995; Wehemeyer 1996). The ability to make choices is considered a vital component of such an empowerment curriculum (Newton, Horner and Lund 1991; Parsons and Reid 1990). A growing literature suggests that access to choice making should be available to all individuals, regardless of their level of impairment (Bannerman *et al.* 1990; Gothelf *et al.* 1994; Kennedy and Haring 1993; Williams 1991). Stalker and Harris (1998) asserted that, compared with the general population, people with learning impairments experience restricted choice-making opportunities and several studies have shown that their opportunities to make choices in educational settings may be limited (Houghton, Bronicki and Guess 1987; Rowland 1990; Sigafoos *et al.* 1994b).

In addition to the exercise of choice being viewed as a fundamental right for people with learning disabilities, the positive effects of making choices on observed levels of engagement and co-operation have been highlighted. For example, Dyer (1989) found that children with autism made substantially more spontaneous requests when they had access to preferred materials compared to non-preferred materials. At a more fundamental level, few experiences are more empowering than having one's choices and decisions respected (Powers *et al.* 1996).

Abery and Zajac (1996) conceptualized the process of achieving self-determination as a developmental one, which should begin for people with impairments, as for everyone, in childhood. They highlighted the fact that if parents and professionals wish to encourage the growth of self-determination in adulthood for people with impairments, the best strategy is to provide many opportunities to practise the necessary skills from an early age. Children in our study were regularly offered choices in a number of situations; choices that, crucially, adults respected. Here are some examples:

- At snack time, a range of choices was available between different types of snack and drinks.

- During a painting activity, children were offered a number of choices throughout the session. They chose which colour paper to use, what sort of equipment to apply paint with and what colour paint to use. One child made 12 such choices during a 15-minute session.

- In one classroom, children were able to choose, by pointing, in what order to do tasks during a 1:1 individual work session.

- In another classroom, children could choose which child to walk to the dining room with at lunchtime.

Below, we list possible questions, which may help staff to reflect on the nature of choice-making opportunities currently being offered to children in their classrooms.

- How often are choices offered?

- What kinds of choices are presented? Material, social, temporal? Material choices relate to opportunities to choose between items of food, to choose between tasks, or to choose equipment to complete a task. Social choices relate to choice of partner (adult or child) – for example, choosing whom to sit next to on the bus, to walk with down the corridor, etc. Temporal choices relate to length of participation in a particular activity (for example choosing to stop looking at one book and look at another, or choosing when to finish painting).

- What factors influence the provision of choice-making opportunities in day-to-day school situations: pragmatic factors such as time; the child's ability; the nature of activity, etc.?

- How are choices presented to children (differentiation aspects according to child ability – e.g. objects of reference; photos or words etc.; are changes in presentation of choice necessary as children's abilities develop)?

- What are the issues surrounding responding positively or otherwise to child expressed choices?

- How are children taught to choose?

- Are there other choices that could be offered?

It is important that children are provided with choices which are as meaningful as possible to them. For example, children should have the opportunity to choose between two preferred activities, as well as between one preferred and one non-preferred activity.

Responding to Spontaneous Communication: Practice Dilemmas

There are likely to be several significant dilemmas involved in providing choices for children with disabilities, as for all children. Children may always choose the same adult to work with or the same activity to work on. This certainly presents challenges, particularly when working with children with autism who may develop very strong preferences. These are matters for discussion and experimentation, however, rather than reasons for not offering the choices – particularly in the light of the research cited above which suggests that children with autism are likely to be much more engaged in activities of their own choosing.

Practitioners in our study discussed issues relating to when it is appropriate to respond to child initiations and when it is less so. Concerns were expressed that all spontaneous communication could not or should not be responded to for a number of reasons. For example, it would be neither advisable nor practicable for children to have unlimited access to preferred food or activities. One teacher argued that it was important to respond positively to spontaneous communication where possible when children were just beginning to communicate intentionally and spontaneously. She talked about her approach to responding to the early spontaneous communication of Rebecca, a child in our study:

> The week Rebecca really progressed dramatically using photographs was when we had very few children in because a lot were on holiday and we had the staff therefore to take her off, to do the things she wanted…we felt that as she was *just* learning to communicate – the more often we could meet her needs then the more she would realize how useful communication was…and hopefully use it more often.

We would support this view. Where at all possible, children at these early stages of communication development must experience the direct benefits of their communication to encourage them to continue in their attempts to get their messages across. Once children's communication abilities are firmly established, however, a time will come when they must learn that adults cannot acquiesce to all requests. Rebecca's teacher found that when other children had returned from holiday, it was no longer practically possible to respond to all of her requests to go to the ball pool. The teacher's strategy was to introduce Rebecca to the concept of waiting for her chosen activity by showing her a photograph of what had to be done before she could have access to it:

> She learnt remarkably quickly…she showed us the photograph of the ball pool one day and we told her 'no, work first', and showed her the work photograph. [*At this point Rebecca became very upset but staff were quickly able to guide her through the completion of a short task that was well within her capabilities.*] She then got to the ball pool for a few minutes a very short period of time after she'd done that work. The second day she brought us the photograph of the ball pool again and we said 'no, work first' and showed her the [work] photograph – she did the work without resisting. The third day she brought us the photograph of work and as soon as she'd finished it she went to show us the photograph of the ball pool.

In this instance, Rebecca's spontaneous communication was responded to, but not immediately. To safeguard children's ongoing development as communicators, it will be important to ensure that a significant proportion of their communications continue to be effective in accessing their needs and wants.

Another teacher in our study expressed the view that it was sometimes necessary to override some of the children's protests in the short term to enable them to experience activities that they may subsequently come to enjoy:

> There's always this balance between responding positively to behaviours that are communication based for positive reasons and not responding to communications that are 'opt out' or 'being frightened' of what's going to happen because 'I don't really understand it'.

As discussed above in the section relating to responding to children's protests, there are a number of careful judgements for practitioners to make regarding under what circumstances to accept or override children's protests in certain situations. If children continue to protest over long periods, then perhaps changes need to be made to the nature of the activity. Tasks could be individualized to take more account of children's own interests. For example, one teacher in our study was successful in enabling children to undertake practice in the area of fine motor skills by laminating a picture of their favourite cartoon character, punching holes in it and making it into a threading activity.

From Communication Opportunities to True Spontaneous Communication

It is vital to keep in mind that the ultimate aim is to enable children to communicate spontaneously in unstructured situations, where adults do not already know what children are going to communicate about. This is the true test of the success of any teaching programme in this area. It is therefore crucial that practitioners are constantly monitoring children's progress towards this goal. A key teaching point is to ensure that there are enough less structured sessions where children have real opportunities to communicate in a truly spontaneous way – for example, in the playground, in the swimming pool, during soft play sessions, in free choice sessions, and so on.

Summary Points

- To enable children such as those in our study to become effective communicators, it is vital to provide them with frequent, high quality opportunities for communication.
- Children should have opportunities to learn how to communicate for a variety of purposes.
- Children's spontaneous communication should be responded to positively as often as possible, practicable and appropriate, particularly in the early stages of their development as spontaneous communicators.
- The ultimate aim is for children to be able to communicate spontaneously in unstructured sessions where adults do not know what they are going to communicate about.

8

Facilitating Interaction Between Children with Autism

The development of peer interaction is recognised as vitally important in the social development of all children (Hartup 1999). Literature on enabling children with autism to interact with their peers has focused almost exclusively on fostering interactions between children with autism and children in mainstream schools. Children with autism and minimal or no speech, however, are often placed in specialist classes, where most of their contact is with other children with autism. Our findings provide some cause for optimism in the area of enabling children with autism to interact with each other.

Key Research Findings

1. Some spontaneous interactions were observed between the children in our study.

2. Most of these interactions related to the taking of equipment or toys from other children.

3. Some interactions of a more social nature were also observed.

4. Children were often directed to sit in a group for a number of sessions, such as snack time, for example. In these

sessions, children were close but not directly interacting with each other.

5.   Beyond this first stage of developing tolerance of the proximity of other children, we observed some effective structured teaching whose aim was to encourage children to interact directly with each other.

A Continuum of Peer Interaction

The use of a developmental approach to the fostering of interaction between children with autism with little or no speech is indicated by our findings; beginning with transactional types of exchange and moving on towards more socially based interactions.

Grabbing

We observed several instances of children with autism trying to take things from each other, by grabbing toys or snacks. These types of interactions were mostly viewed as undesirable by the classroom staff who usually intervened promptly to curtail them, understandably fearing that children might become distressed if the situation were allowed to develop further. Such types of interaction, however, are typical of young children and seen as important for the development of early negotiation skills. Schaffer (1996), while cautioning that peer relationships can be culturally specific, indicated that a developmental trend could be discerned. Infants have difficulty in linking their behaviour to that of their peers well into the second year of life. By the age of two, however, social play predominates over solitary play and continues to develop rapidly during the preschool years. Although children as young as 20 months can adapt their behaviour according to their interactive partner, when conflicts arise they can often react in quite stereotypical ways. Understandably, older children too experience greater social difficulty in conflict rather than non-conflict situations.

Given that resolution of peer conflicts is, therefore, a developmental issue, we suggested to Anna, a classroom assistant, that she might wait longer before intervening in these 'snatch-and-grab' types of interactions. While carefully monitoring the situation, we suggested that she give children both the opportunity to experience the peer interaction, as well as practice in negotiation. Anna reported that she had tried 'stepping back' when these exchanges occurred and found that on several occasions the children had managed to resolve the situation, at a simple level, without necessarily resorting to aggression (e.g. letting go of the toy or holding onto it until the other child gave up). Children did seem to be monitoring each other's reactions during these interactions, rather than focusing only on the object desired. Obviously, at a practical level, close adult supervision is vital in such situations.

Giving and Receiving Items

We observed some effective structured sessions, in which staff engineered opportunities for children to give and receive items (Box 8.1).

Box 8.1

Practice Scenario: Passing the Hat

One teacher sat her children in a semi-circle and sang a 'hello' song to the first child, putting a large hat on his head. Then at the end of the verse, she prompted this child to put the hat onto the head of the child sitting next to him and so on. Children were actively co-operating and enjoying this session within a few weeks. The teacher began to substitute the hat with other items to try to maintain the children's interest – for example, scarves, large glasses, necklaces, shawls, bracelets, glittery wigs, and so on.

Another situation in which children were prompted to give and receive things was at snack times, where they were prompted to give and take mats, cups and plates.

Turn-Taking Games

The ability to take turns is a key element in social development (Nind and Hewett 1994). Literature in the area of autism has rightly focused on children's ability to take communicative turns with an adult (Christie *et al.* 1992; Prevezer 1990) since adults can provide the necessary social scaffolding for such interactions more easily (see Chapter 4). Teaching children with autism how to take turns with other children with autism has rarely been the focus of research, although it does form an important issue for practitioners. In Box 8.2 we describe how one teacher successfully engineered a simple turn-taking game between two children in our study.

Box 8.2

Practice Scenario: Turns with the Helter-Skelter

Two children were prompted to take turns putting a ball down a helter-skelter toy, each child having the skill and motivation to play with this toy alone. Initially, physical prompts were necessary to encourage the children to wait for their turn. Gradually, the teacher was able to reduce these prompts, as they learnt the rules of the game. Eventually, they were able to sustain a short period of turn taking without the teacher's help. Importantly, this teacher used very little speech throughout this scenario, thus allowing the children to concentrate wholly on what was happening. Learning to take turns with another child is challenging enough for children with autism, without adding the further difficulty of the adult facilitator using speech, which they are unlikely to understand. The key enabling factors in this scenario were thought to be:

- the simplicity of the game
- the use of equipment motivating to both children
- the use of a minimal speech approach
- reducing physical prompts
- the predictability of the game
- the clarity of the nature of the role for each child.

These enabling factors could be applied to a range of other simple activities, for example, completing the final stages of a floor puzzle. A key teaching point is that the focus of the activity is learning to take turns so the activity itself must be simple, motivating and predictable. Activities chosen should be familiar ones so that children do not have to expend effort mastering novel cognitive components of the tasks themselves. Other activities found to be successful in supporting quality interactions between children such as those in our study included the following:

- Teach two children how to wind themselves together (by physical prompts or modelling but using little speech) from the two ends of a sari or long piece of material. The anticipation of meeting in the middle often creates much amusement! When children are familiar with the activity, each child could be taught how to communicate 'go' to the other.

- Seat two children with a large tray (lined with paper) across both their knees, place balls or marbles dipped in paint into the tray and show the children how to tip the tray in various directions to make tracks on the paper.

- Teach two children to use a seesaw – the children are quick to realize how ineffectual a seesaw is with only them on it!

Social Games: Modelling Peer Interaction

We observed a few social interactions of a more spontaneous nature between some children in our study. The interaction described in Box 8.3 was remarkable, not only because of the degree of spontaneity evident but also because of the mutual enjoyment that each child apparently derived from the experience.

Box 8.3

Practice Scenario: Helena Playing with Claire

A relatively complex spontaneous social interaction between two children with autism occurred in the playground immediately after an adult (Laura) had finished playing a simple Proximal Communication game with Helena, one of the children in the study.

The game consisted of Laura pulling Helena towards her quickly, using a rising vocalization (aaaaa!!) and then tickling her and laughing with her. Helena would then walk backwards and hold out her hands to indicate that she wanted to continue. Laura was trying to foster intentional use of eye gaze, by waiting for Helena to look at her before continuing with the game, which she soon began to do.

Claire, a verbal child with autism, was watching the game with interest. Helena was thoroughly enjoying the game and was very eager to continue with it. Since the end of playtime was approaching, Laura began to wind down the game, by gradually responding less vigorously. Helena sensed the change and wandered off.

She then approached Claire, and held out her hands to her, clearly indicating that she wanted to continue with the same game. Claire took Helena's hands and began to shake them up and down, laughing loudly as she had seen Laura doing. Helena was clearly enjoying herself and initiated this game with Claire on two more occasions in the next ten minutes.

Helena had not made any requests for social interaction on the day of shadowing and yet she was able to engage another child with autism in a social interaction on three occasions in a ten-minute interval. Can we identify aspects of the situation that had enabled her to do so? We believe that the following factors were important:

- the simplicity of the game itself

- the fun element of the game which clearly appealed to both children

- the dramatic aspect of the game, introduced by the sudden and vigorous pulling of Helena by the hands, followed by rigorous tickling
- the use of a pause/burst approach (see Chapter 4) which made it clear when it was Helena's turn to communicate
- Laura's exaggerated facial expressions and vocalizations (enthusiastic laughter)
- the minimal use of speech
- the clearly defined roles within the game – someone pulls and someone is pulled
- the fact that Claire was a verbal child with autism who apparently experienced fewer social difficulties than Helena may also have been a contributory factor to the success of the interaction.

It may be possible, therefore, to promote interaction between children with autism using modelling, where simple roles for each child are demonstrated within the game. This is an approach that clearly warrants further exploration.

Modelling Peer Interaction: The Use of Books

We also observed some very interesting unplanned interactions between children with autism centred on books. These interactions occurred, again, as a result of unintentional modelling by classroom staff in the context of the storytelling session referred to in Chapter 3. The children were encouraged to sit in a circle while the stories were read. Stories such as 'What's the Time Mr Wolf?' were read in a very exaggerated way, with much use of exaggerated facial expression and slowing down of speech to create maximum anticipation. On the line, 'It's dinnertime!!' the teacher would run quickly around the group and tickle each child vigorously. Most of the children responded extremely well to this, wriggling *in anticipation* of the tickle. An unexpected result of these sessions was the way in which three children began to imitate the role of the storytelling adult outside these sessions. During a period when children looked at the books independently, we observed three children with autism approach and tickle other children while looking at the 'What's the Time Mr Wolf?' book.

It would appear here, as in the scenario above, that the key elements which attracted and motivated children in the teacher's storytelling performance were:

- the use of exaggeration and pantomime
- the clarity of her role
- the predictability of role
- the fun generated by this combination.

We would suggest that the deliberate use of modelling strategies might be a powerful strategy in enabling children to interact with each other. What is being provided is a 'social script' for the children to follow. It would appear that children with autism and difficulties in understanding speech are able to follow such scripts when they are comprehensible, predictable and enjoyable enough. Sherratt (1999) has described the successful use of a modelling strategy in enabling children with autism to engage spontaneously in symbolic play.

Spontaneous Proximal Communication between Siblings with Autism

As part of our long-term follow-up of some of the children from the present study, we were able to videotape two brothers, both with autism and minimal speech, engaging in protracted bouts of spontaneous Proximal Communication. Both showed clear pleasure in each other's company and in the activity. They were very skilful in play wrestling each other in a way that was energetic but safe. This remarkable data is currently being analysed in further detail.

Programmes to Encourage Interaction Between Children

An Audio-Movement Programme

We observed the effective use of an audio programme linked to movement in one classroom to promote direct interaction between children. The programme consists of audiotapes, which are graded according to complexity and length. Within the programme, particular sounds on the audiotapes are linked to particular movements. For example, sandpaper being rubbed was the sound that instructed children to rub their hands together. In the first instance, adults needed to model or prompt the movement but children quickly learnt to recognize which movement was associated with which sound. One key enabling aspect of this programme was that children did not have to understand speech to know what to do next. The sounds themselves acted as non-verbal prompts. This non-verbal associative form of presentation appears particularly well suited to the learning style of children such as those in our study. The sounds themselves were rhythmical, clear and attention getting. At the end of each section, the spoken word 'stop' clearly informed children to stop what they were doing and wait for the next sound.

Once children were familiar with sounds and actions, they could be encouraged to sit in pairs and rub each other's hands and feet, etc. Again, the structure, predictability and enjoyable nature of the activity appeared to enable children to engage in simple interactions with other children.

The Use of Laban Activities

Veronica Sherborne's (1990) easily accessible manual of Laban activities is another approach which, we suggest, can be successfully used to enable children to interact with each other in structured and enjoyable situations. This book provides a clear rationale for the use of graded interaction activities, designed to be particularly enjoyable for young children. For example, an early activity has children on all fours, side by side to form a tunnel, which another child is then encouraged to crawl through. Such activities can be introduced gradually, with adults perhaps forming a bigger and more stable tunnel initially with children being encouraged to join the tunnel later on.

Summary Points

- Children with autism and little or no speech can and do interact with each other, when adults are able to provide enjoyable, predictable and structured situations in which they can learn to do so.

- The development of interactions between children with autism is an important area which is likely to require a continuum approach from establishing tolerance of the proximity of other children, through simple giving and receiving interactions within structured activities, to more complex social interactions as described above.

9

Enabling Styles
of Classroom Management

It is universally accepted that the rate and quality of children's learning in schools, including levels of child engagement and the development of communication abilities, are significantly enhanced by the use of effective classroom management approaches (Jones and Warren 1991).

Key research findings

1. Key aspects of a communication-enabling classroom management approach were found to be: effective deployment of staff; effective training of staff; effective management of time; clear goals for individual sessions based on specific long-term objectives.

2. Children communicated most when they were engaged in an activity that they were enjoying *and* had access to an adult employing communication-enabling strategies.

Use of Staff

The issue of deployment of staff in classrooms for children with disabilities has often been explored. Ware (1994), for example, discussed the use of room management in which each member of staff has a specific role within the classroom, namely the room manager, a 1:1 worker and someone to deal with practical problems arising.

Teachers in our study were all keenly aware of the need to identify roles for every member of staff during each activity throughout the day. Use of staff changed according to the pattern of teaching activities being undertaken at any given time. For example, in one classroom during a morning session, the teacher and one assistant worked with children individually on cognitive tasks, while the second classroom assistant supervised those children who were not engaged in individual work in a free choice session. In another classroom, during an observed period, one member of staff was responsible for overseeing independent work, while the second engaged in an individual Proximal Communication session and the third oversaw the rest of the children. These systems reached maximum effectiveness when a number of children were able to work independently. In one classroom three children could complete tasks without help in a TEACCH independent work session, overseen by one adult who was monitoring their levels of engagement. This efficient use of staff became more difficult on days when, for whatever reason, children were unable or reluctant to work through tasks independently.

In all of the classrooms, the most difficult role was often that of the member of staff who was overseeing a group of children who were not being worked with individually. These were the sessions where most disruption could occur, since children found this relatively unstructured time difficult to manage.

In practice, the deployment of staff in classrooms for children with autism involves constant skilful monitoring by the teacher who has to make many rapid decisions throughout the course of the day about who should be doing what with whom. The length of time in which children engage in activities can be unpredictable, necessitating flexibility in planning, within an overall clear structure.

Using Staff to Maximize Opportunities for Spontaneous Communication

We observed a number of occasions where staff deployment could have been more effective. One such scenario is detailed in Box 9.1, together with suggestions for improvement.

Box 9.1

Practice Scenario: A Drinks Session

Setting the Scene

- Six children were sitting around two rectangular tables pushed together.

- Two members of staff were going around the table, one offering the children drinks, while the other followed offering crisps or biscuits.

The Effects on Child Communication

- Children were clearly distracted by the activity of the two adults.

- The pace of the session was very quick, as staff tried to keep up with each other and get around the group before children became bored or restless. This meant that the creation of communication opportunities for children could be given little time or thought.

- Because of this, most communications were prompted either physically or verbally.

- Some children became agitated because of the speed of the process – one child was offered crisps, still having a mouth full of juice.

Staff Comments on the Session

- The teacher involved commented afterwards that the session had felt very 'rushed'. She said that she felt she was always trying to 'catch up' with the session, rather than guiding it in the way that she wanted.

Suggestions for Change

- Having discussed these issues with the classroom team, we suggested the following changes to the deployment of staff:

  - Divide the children into two groups of three.

  - Locate these groups so that they are not visible to each other, if possible, to minimize distractions.

  - Compose each group of children in such a way as to maximize communication opportunities. For example, place children with particularly short concentration spans in different groups.

  - The member of staff should be positioned so that she can monitor all of the children's spontaneous communications.

Potential Benefits of this Approach

- The benefits of substituting a 2:6 staffing ratio with 1:3 staffing can be many. Immediately the communicative environment becomes more structured and predictable for the children.

- The presence of one adult clarifies for children who their communication partner is going to be, a vital consideration for children with very significant communication difficulties.

- Adults are better able to monitor children's communication attempts in a smaller group where there are fewer distractions.

- The pace of the session becomes easier to manage since only one adult is involved and the number of children is halved.

- The smaller group means that children's communicative attempts may be more quickly and accurately responded to.

Staff Feedback on the Changes

- Both adults felt that the drinks session was much more productive in terms of communication after the division of the group into two.

- Children quickly became familiar with the changes and spontaneously went to their own seats in the new locations after only a few days.

We returned to the classroom to video the newly organized drinks sessions and found that children were communicating much more than in the whole class grouping. In the space of two minutes, three children communicated a total of thirteen times.

Classroom Management and Levels of Engagement

McGhee *et al.* (1991) argued that because 'early intervention must be accomplished within a relatively short time frame, it is important to secure engagement and responsiveness to teaching contacts as quickly as possible' (p.44). They highlighted the particular challenges posed by children with autism, who are likely to be much less engaged than other children.

Before learning can occur, adults must try to ensure that children with autism are actively engaged with their environment for as much of the time as possible. Dyer (1989) indicated that children engaged most when they were participating in activities of their own choosing while Peck (1985) found that students with autism spontaneously communicated more when they were given greater control over aspects of their environments.

Planning for Maximum Engagement

Children with autism and very limited speech often experience significant difficulties in co-ordinating their attention. A very important classroom management issue to be addressed, therefore, is how maximum levels of engagement can be achieved for the majority of these children on a daily basis.

Teachers were aware of the need to organize low arousal areas in various areas in the classroom to provide optimum working conditions for children. In one classroom, moveable dividers were used to screen off specific areas of the classroom: one section for one-to-one tabletop work; another for unstructured play; a third for group activities and finally a designated area for Proximal Communication sessions. In general, this division of space worked well. In another classroom, the bottom section of the window in the quiet area was painted over to block out distractions.

From our observations, it appeared that many children were quite severely affected by the sudden and unpredictable noises of other children. Several children attempted to block out such noises by putting their fingers in their ears. These are extremely difficult issues to deal with at a practical level. We did observe, however, that the likelihood of such distractions developing is significantly reduced when high levels of engagement are achieved for as many of the children as possible. Several staff reported improvements in this context after the introduction of the TEACCH structured teaching approach.

Effective Use of Time:
A Small Group Teaching Approach

Achieving maximum engagement for the maximum number of children requires skilful deployment of staff and the effective use of small group activities on the timetable, so that one member of staff is working with more than one child at a time. This is essential since, as we have seen, it is neither practicable nor necessarily advisable for children to have 1:1 teaching for the whole school day.

One of the scenarios we aimed to video in each classroom was a group teaching activity. Interestingly, this proved difficult, since few such sessions occurred in some of the classrooms taking part. There were a number of reasons for this. First, the average age of the children in the study was 4.5 years, with the majority having been in full-time education for less than one year. In practice, this meant that many of the children were at the early stages of interacting successfully with an adult, even on an individual basis.

Clearly intensive periods of individual tuition are necessary for children at these early stages to develop relationships, and communication abilities as well as cognitive and self-help skills. We did observe some sessions, however, which suggested that young children with autism and minimal speech could learn in small and sometimes larger groups. Effective group learning sessions were most likely to occur when the adults used communication-enabling approaches.

A Lotto Game

One of the most successful group sessions that we observed occurred when four children played sound lotto, supported by two adults, the children having been gradually introduced to this activity over a number of days. When the game was first introduced, children were helped to match the sounds to the pictures quickly so that the game was relatively short, lasting only three or four minutes. Pace of sessions is critical to ensure child engagement in new activities. If sessions are too slow when they are first introduced, children may lose interest and be reluctant to engage in the activity when it is next introduced.

Once the children were familiar with the structure of the game, adults began to slow it down, giving more time for the children to listen to the sounds and match them to pictures with less help. Other children were able to wait for their turn more easily, knowing that their turn would come. Another key teaching strategy here was the use of a minimal speech approach. Adults merely showed the child where the counter should go without speaking or later by simply saying 'car'. Eventually, communication opportunities were introduced into the session. For example, children chose which board they wanted at the start of the session and then communicated spontaneously to an adult, generally by the use of multipointing, which sound matched which picture.

It is interesting, from a theoretical perspective, that these children all had little or no speech and extreme difficulty in understanding spoken language and yet were rapidly able to distinguish a wide range of environmental sounds. This issue clearly warrants further investigation.

Group Story Time

We have referred to this story activity previously. Here we want to emphasize the success of the session as a group teaching activity. All of the children were of pre-school age and attended the nursery for only two days a week. The high level of concentration apparent during these 15-minute sessions was remarkable. Three or four short stories were read each day, with the same stories being read nearly every day to provide predictability and develop anticipation. Within these sessions children were learning many valuable lessons, such as how to concentrate in a group and how to enjoy themselves within this social setting.

Circle Rhymes

In two classrooms, we observed successful singing sessions in which a group of children sat on chairs in a circle while each child had a turn at participating in the song. The key point to mention here is that in both classrooms the children remained engaged for at least a five-minute period, having learned to wait for their turn. The concrete prompts (passing around of a hat, etc.) seemed important in giving them a visual cue as to what was happening and when it would be their turn. In one classroom, David, a child in our study was particularly reluctant to participate and repeatedly made loud wailing noises when brought to the group. The teacher compromised with him by allowing him to join the group at the end when it was his turn. David kept a close eye on the proceedings from a distance and appeared in his seat just at the moment when it was his turn! When this activity was observed at a later date, David had become a member of the group, albeit a somewhat reluctant one.

A Group Painting Activity

Another effective group activity we observed was a painting session in which four or five children stood around a table and painted onto a large and heavy cardboard sheet (6ft x 3ft) which covered the table. We suggested this activity to the class team, based on our own experience. The teacher in this classroom had commented that children generally spent very little time painting on the small sheets of sugar paper often used in painting sessions. She also pointed out that the paper often disintegrated under the impact of the water based paints and vigorous brushwork; hence the suggestion that large sheets of thick cardboard be used which are often readily available in schools in the form of cardboard delivery cartons.

This board-painting activity was ongoing with the same piece of card being brought out every week. On each occasion, a particular range of related colours (e.g. dark green, light green, etc., along with tonal agents such as white, yellow ochre and a small amount of black) were on offer, from which the children could choose. The next week a different range of colours, along with the same tonal agents, was introduced. In this way the children were able to explore the nature of the tonal and colour effects, without ending up with the inevitable muddy brown which results from mixing a wide range of colours together at the same time.

Children also had the option of choosing from a range of tools with which to work on the card. Occasionally, the teacher gave children sand to alter the texture of the paint (to which a small amount of PVA glue had been added to aid adhesion). As the weeks went on it became clear to us, as observers, that as soon as the children saw the card being put on the table they had a set of clear expectations about the nature of the activity. In effect, as well as the many other benefits of this session, the children needed less staff support during this activity over time. Two adults were successfully able to create communication opportunities for all the children during this session. Most of the time the children painted in parallel, but occasionally more than one child would contribute towards painting the same area. The key enabling factors in this situation appeared to be:

- familiarity of the activity
- predictability
- motivation supported by many choices throughout the activity
- minimal speech use by staff.

The absence of any predefined end product in this art activity allowed the children to focus on the process and communicate spontaneously when they wanted to.

Getting changed for PE

One classroom teacher created many opportunities for communication within a 1:3 staffing ratio, as children changed for a session in the ball pool, in the following way:

- An adult sat opposite the children who sat in a small semi-circle.

- She waited until the children realized that they needed help getting dressed or undressed and then she responded to their spontaneous communication.

- If she believed that children were not yet able to initiate the communication, she prompted it, using a minimal speech approach combined with multipointing. For example, children were physically prompted to point first to themselves and then to their own shoes or whatever item they needed help with.

- When children were getting dressed, the member of staff created problem-solving activities by holding up two items of clothing and waiting for children to indicate which one needed to be put on next, again using a minimal speech approach. So instead of saying 'Which one do you need next?', the teacher simply held up the items and waited. If children did not respond, then the teacher would physically prompt them to point to the correct item, saying emphatically 'vest', for example.

Important underlying practice points supporting the success of this communication-enabling session would seem to be as follows:

- Children understood the parameters of the activity.

- The predictability of the interaction scenario was signalled by the nature of the activity and the position of chairs.

- A minimal speech approach was adopted.

- Time was allowed for children to realize that they had a need.

- Communicative behaviours appropriate to the children's development level were targeted.

TEACCH and Spontaneous Communication

The management of classrooms for children with autism in the UK has been significantly affected in recent years by the structured teaching approach developed by Division TEACCH (Schopler, Mesibov and Hearsey 1995). Key elements of the approach are physical organization; timetables; independent work and the implementation of a number of predictable routines. There is little doubt that structured teaching has a significant role in rendering environments comprehensible to students with autism and TEACCH is particularly effective in enabling such students to work independently.

Although the many benefits of structured teaching are clearly acknowledged, a few concerns have been raised about the limitations of the approach. For example, Jordan and Powell (1997) commented that while structured teaching may effectively organize the curriculum and the environment for pupils with autism, individuals become dependent on this structure, since the system does not provide pupils with 'internally cued strategies' (p.20) which might ultimately lead to independence from it.

Little has been written on the important subject of the relationship between structured teaching and the development of spontaneous communication in children with autism. Svavarsdottir (1992) conducted one such small-scale study in the context of three classrooms in North Carolina. The effects of the various dimensions of structured teaching on spontaneous communication were examined and a number of interesting issues were highlighted. It was found that the use of high dividers to mark boundaries within the classroom sometimes prevented adults from seeing when children were trying to get attention. Svavarsdottir noted that the timetable was a 'powerful instrument' in all three classrooms observed, but that it often formed the only subject for communication, evidenced by the fact that most interactions occurred around the timetable in change-over periods.

The use of TEACCH routines (daily, work and interactive) appeared to provide few opportunities for spontaneous communication, since the daily and work routines focused on children becoming independent in a number of behavioural sequences, while interactive routines were conducted through question and answer sessions. Svavarsdottir's overall conclusion was that in the three TEACCH classrooms observed most of the children's communications were in the form of responses to teacher elicitations. In the light of this finding, the effect of the use of structured teaching on the development of spontaneous communication needs careful consideration.

Promoting Spontaneous Communication Within a TEACCH Context

With careful planning, spontaneous communication can certainly develop in a classroom where a structured teaching approach is in use. To a large extent, the TEACCH approach is content free: teachers choose which activities go to make up the timetable. Within those activities, a range of communication-enabling approaches such as those described throughout this book can be adopted. Proximal Communication sessions can be timetabled, for example, along with group activities such as painting or PE sessions, during which many opportunities for children to practise spontaneous communication abilities can be created. The inclusion of 'choice' sessions on the timetable can give children the opportunity to make real decisions about what they want to do at such times. The only session which may preclude the use of spontaneous communication abilities is the independent work session, where the primary aim is for children to work through a number of activities without help.

A key issue is the extent to which teachers regard the development of spontaneous communication as a central aim of their educational approach. We would argue strongly that since communication development constitutes such an important goal for these children, enabling spontaneity should be very high on the educational agenda.

Timetables and Spontaneity

Like Svavarsdottir (1992), we found that the use of the timetable was a critical component of classroom management approaches in our five classrooms. In four of the five classrooms, the timetable was displayed as a pictorial sequence of events. We would stress the importance of checking that children actually understand the timetable through careful assessment of children's reactions to individual symbols or pictures. Generally, because of teachers' obviously well-founded beliefs about the need to provide structure and predictability for these children, timetables were followed fairly precisely. However, one teacher in our study, Sue, identified the tension between providing structure and predictability and the need to respond to children's spontaneous communications. She felt that there were occasions when the timetable should be used more flexibly. For example, when children were at the early stages of learning to communicate, she was prepared to modify the timetable in favour of activities which children spontaneously communicated that they wanted to do next. For example, she was just about to tell children that it was drinks time when Rebecca, a child in our study, spontaneously asked to use play dough by pointing to it in a cupboard. Since Rebecca was just beginning to point and this was one of the first occasions when she had used this skill in a completely unstructured situation, Sue decided to have a play dough session. In order to have the flexibility to make changes to the timetable, Sue communicated about forthcoming activities just before they were about to occur, rather than going through forthcoming activities in a circle time situation as some teachers did.

This more flexible approach to the timetable may have other benefits. Over-strict adherence to a class timetable may serve to exacerbate children's own rigid behaviour patterns. This is a perspective that seems worthy of further exploration, given the significant emphasis currently placed on timetables in classroom management for children with autism.

In another classroom, children were able to make spontaneous choices about activities by taking a symbol stuck with velcro to a wall-mounted card and giving it to an adult. One child began to make frequent spontaneous choices using these symbols within weeks of first attending the pre-school class. Most importantly, his choices were always accepted in these early stages of his communicative development.

Summary Points

- The ways in which the classrooms in our study were managed significantly affected the extent to which they supported a communication-enabling environment.

- Effective deployment of staff and grouping of children were found to be especially important factors.

- Children were able to develop spontaneous communication abilities in the context of small groups, when staff used a range of communication enabling strategies.

Communication within the Curriculum

This chapter explores the relationship between the curricular emphasis on the development of communication and social abilities that we are advocating and the current educational framework in the UK.

Key Research Findings

- Teachers believed that communication was the most important curricular area for the children in our study.

- Teachers felt strongly that the current curricular framework, with its emphasis on the National Curriculum, does not adequately address the learning needs of children with autism and little or no speech.

The National Curriculum: What Teachers Said

Teachers generally felt that they had to try to 'fit the children into the National Curriculum' because it did not encompass the learning needs of the children they taught in many ways. One teacher commented that although there had been attempts to broaden the National Curriculum for children with learning impairments, she continued to feel that the National Curriculum was a 'top-down rather than bottom-up' approach, focusing on the delivery of a prescribed curriculum, rather than on the needs of individual children.

Another teacher argued that the National Curriculum was 'far too prescriptive' as well as being 'at far too high a level' and was 'not looking at children's needs'. Teachers talked about 'playing with words' and 'tokenism' in connection with accountability frameworks: 'We shouldn't have to pretend that we're doing History when we're looking at pointing to a sequence of cards.'

The tension between the need for extensive communication teaching and the need visibly to deliver a broad and balanced curriculum, discussed by Hewett and Nind (1998), was also identified by one of our participants: 'Is it not a more basic *right* to learn to communicate...to learn to interact? And if that takes three-quarters of the time given for the curriculum then I feel that's important and it should not be balanced – it should be teaching the skills the children need.'

The National Curriculum: Critiques

Significant concerns continue to be expressed, both generally and in relation to children with special educational needs, regarding the central role of the National Curriculum in our educational system. At a moral level, Kelly (1994) referred to the worrying erosion of democratic discussion in the field of education in the UK, asserting that since the National Curriculum has become the dominant ideology 'it does not have to justify its educational values because it is able to control the degree to which they will be discussed and determine what counts as true' (p.12). From a different, although equally disturbing perspective, Quicke (1999) argued strongly that the Education Reform Act of 1988 'has not resulted in the development of a curriculum which can meet the needs of young persons at the end of the twentieth century' (p.12), since it has completely failed to enhance the development of personal autonomy or social commitment essential for the development of a 'learning society' (p.vii). These are major criticisms that have yet to be addressed in any significant way by governmental policy makers.

Despite a reduction in curriculum content, resulting from the Dearing Report (SCAA 1994), and subsequent revisions, the National Curriculum's subject-based format continues to appear significantly at odds with the process model of curriculum accepted by many as fundamental in the area of special educational needs (Halpin and Lewis 1996).

Several educationalists have argued that, far from enhancing educational opportunities for children with severe disabilities, the National Curriculum may have resulted in significant disadvantage for some children (Jordan and Powell 1992). Carpenter and Ashdown (1996) observed that many teachers continued to believe that the National Curriculum focused on average children in mainstream schools and was not an appropriate vehicle for the teaching of children with a range of impairment. Similarly Lloyd (1997) found that many teachers perceived it as 'narrowly prescriptive, relevant for only a minority of children' (p.175). Jordan and Powell (1997) argued that key problems posed for those educating children with autism within the National Curriculum relate to time constraints and priority issues that the National Curriculum presents. They contended that pupils with autism need significant amounts of teaching in areas which lie outside the National Curriculum, such as communication and social abilities.

The situation is not helped by guidance that appears contradictory. Some aspects of official documentation appear to advocate a central position for the notion of responding to the individual needs of the child: 'Planning starts from the basis of needs, interests and aptitudes and achievements of the pupils' (SCAA 1996, p.11). However, such a flexible response does not seem to extend so far as to allow teachers to focus on some particularly crucial areas of the curriculum, such as communication, to the exclusion of other areas such as history. While acknowledging individual needs as a starting point, the 1996 SCAA document *Planning the Curriculum for Pupils with Profound and Multiple Learning Difficulties* continues both to discuss the 'prominence' of the National Curriculum in these children's education and to advocate a 'subject-focused' approach. Such mixed messages have frequently resulted in overcrowded curricular programmes for some children with special educational needs and unacceptably high levels of stress for teachers.

Porter, Miller and Pease (1997), in their examination of curriculum access for deaf-blind children, found that little consensus regarding curriculum existed between the 57 teachers questioned. No fewer than 11 additional curricular areas were added to the National Curriculum by these staff to ensure that all children's needs could be met. The authors stressed that 'the curriculum appears fragmented with little way of ensuring continuity and progression' (p.75).

The Revised National Curriculum

The recent review of the National Curriculum (DfEE 1999) appears to offer little clarification of the current position, nor acknowledgement of the continuing difficulties that the National Curriculum poses for teachers of children who are achieving at significantly below age-related expectations. The document focuses on access to content for pupils with special educational needs, rather than the content or priority issues: 'Teachers should teach the skills, knowledge and understanding in the programmes of study in ways appropriate to the abilities of their pupils' (DfEE 1999, p.6).

A new statutory statement on inclusion sets out key principles for schools to consider at all levels of curricular planning:

- setting suitable learning challenges
- responding to pupils' diverse learning needs
- overcoming potential barriers to learning and assessment for individuals and groups of pupils.

These principles do not address the central issue of the appropriateness of the current National Curriculum for children such as those in our study.

The Need for Change

Over a decade after the introduction of The Education Reform Act 1988, many teachers of children with complex learning and language difficulties continue to work under high levels of stress. They are required to teach children with minimal language abilities subjects such as history and geography, which are heavily language based and have complex time and spatial concepts.

Some OFSTED Inspection teams understand the difficulties and do not appear to expect the detailed documentation in this area, for children such as those in our study, but others expect strict adherence to a subject focus. This inconsistent and unacceptable situation should be resolved quickly through the introduction of statutory guidelines that allow teachers the flexibility to make judgements about the appropriateness of particular subjects as learning contexts for their pupils. Some children may progress sufficiently in their language and conceptual development to render the teaching of history and geography meaningful, while for others these subjects may remain inappropriate areas of learning, given the need to maximize their ability to communicate effectively.

The Need for An Inclusive Curriculum

As we argued recently (Whittaker and Potter 1999a), a truly inclusive National Curriculum is necessary to achieve appropriate curricular provision for children such as those in our study. Such a curriculum would include a meaningful focus on core areas such as the development of communication, social skills and self-determination abilities for *all* children, with a flexibility to adapt to individual needs. The inclusive curriculum would end the current unacceptable necessity of attempting to fit children with complex learning needs into a rigid and largely unsuitable curricular framework.

Approaches to Meeting Children's Needs Within the Current Curricular Framework

Given the current situation, what can teachers of children with autism and minimal or no speech do to ensure that a communication curriculum will be acceptable within the existing accountability framework? The following broad guidelines are suggested for use in curricular documentation:

- Include a written, detailed and explicit rationale to justify the emphasis on communication within the curriculum you offer. Include detailed reference to relevant research literature to support your case. Support this curricular decision with helpful official guidance.

- Include a written, detailed and explicit rationale for the use of specific teaching approaches in the area of communication, for example, a minimal speech approach.

- Ensure that you use record-keeping instruments which have the necessary focus, detail and sensitivity to record all of the children's progress in the area of communication. This can be usefully supplemented by dated videotaped evidence, collected on the same activities but over time, so that progress in communication can be easily observed.

Prioritizing Communication in the Curriculum: An Explicit Rationale

A clear policy statement regarding the centrality of communication teaching for children with autism is likely to be most effective if well supported by reference to current research literature. The notion of achieving empowerment for pupils with autism through the development of communication abilities is a fundamental one and needs to be highlighted. Reference to literature reviews and research findings in this and other publications would also provide extensive support for prioritizing communication teaching for this group of children.

An example of what might be contained within such a statement is provided below. Schools will obviously need to develop their own individual statements in order to ensure ownership and commitment to the principles discussed. We would always advise the seeking out of key research papers to ensure that relevant theoretical frameworks are clearly understood.

Sample Rationale

CURRICULAR EMPHASIS ON COMMUNICATION FOR PUPILS WITH
AUTISM AND MINIMAL OR NO SPEECH: A RATIONALE

The right of all children to 'freedom of expression' as a means of ensuring their personal autonomy has been enshrined in Article 13 of the United Nations Convention on the Rights of the Child (1989). Due to the nature of their significant communication impairments, the task of ensuring that children with autism enjoy 'freedom of expression' is a major one, the success of which rests with those who live with the children and those who educate them.

For such a task to be achieved, it is widely recognized and accepted that a curricular emphasis on communication will be essential (Jordan and Powell 1997; Potter and Whittaker 2001; Quill 1995).

Acknowledgement of the need for particular curricular emphases to meet specific individual needs is clearly legislated for within various government guidelines. The document *Planning the Curriculum for Pupils with Profound and Multiple Learning Impairments* (SCAA 1996), stated that:

> The starting point [for curriculum development] must be the needs of the pupil... The priorities identified...may relate to any aspect of the whole curriculum. The priorities identified for a pupil with PMLD will often relate to the skills of communication. (SCAA 1996, p.15)

Additionally, *Planning the Curriculum at Key Stages 1 and 2* (SCAA 1995) emphasized the need to place the National Curriculum within the broader context of the school's overall curricular aims and policies: 'Every school is different and will need to design a curriculum to meet its own particular circumstances' (SCAA 1995, p.27).

In line with such government guidance, we have identified the areas of communication and social development as clear curricular priorities for children with autism. These priorities are reflected in time allocations, classroom management strategies and recording documentation.

Rationale for the Use of Specialist Teaching Approaches

It will be important to provide a clear and explicit rationale for the use of specialist teaching approaches, such as the use of Proximal Communication or a minimal speech approach, for any interested parties, including OFSTED. Such rationales might include the following sections:

- a short definition of the approach

- a concise rationale for use of this approach with particular groups of children with autism, which includes supporting literature

- a few clear examples of the approach in practice

- systems to monitor the effectiveness of the approach.

Example: A Minimal Speech Approach

DEFINITION

A minimal speech approach is one where adults consistently use minimal and conceptually simple speech (one, two or three words) in combination with non-verbal ways of interacting with children who have severe difficulties in understanding spoken language.

A RATIONALE

It is well accepted that many children with autism experience extreme difficulties in understanding speech (Rapin and Dunn 1997; Schopler 1995; Schuler *et al.* 1997). Some researchers have found that these children become distressed or withdraw socially when adults interact with them using too much speech (Klin 1991; Peterson *et al.* 1995; Potter and Whittaker 2001). Potter and Whittaker (2001) [i.e. this book] described how the use of a minimal speech approach, in combination with a range of non-verbal ways of interacting, resulted in greater social response and spontaneous communication in a group of children with autism and severe difficulties understanding speech. They argued that the consistent use of a minimal speech approach allows these children gradually to understand more speech and become more engaged in social interactions.

When using a minimal speech approach, classroom staff aim to interact with children using as little speech as possible. They concentrate on key functional words supported by visual cues where appropriate, as in the example below.

Situation	Everyday speech	A minimal speech approach
Getting ready to go out to play	An adult approaches John and says: 'Come on, John, let's go and get your coat on, it's time to go out to play now.'	An adult approaches John, gains his attention, non-verbally, shows him a picture of the playground and says *only* 'coat' clearly, slowly and with emphasis.

Anonymous examples drawn from the school's own experience should be substituted for this specimen scenario.

MONITORING THE EFFECTIVENESS OF THE APPROACH

The effects of this approach are monitored through careful formal and informal classroom observation and assessment of:

- children's developing understanding of individual words
- their social response in interactions with adults using this approach over time, which could be usefully videotaped.

Spontaneous Communication and Effective Record Keeping

If a curricular emphasis on communication teaching is to be adequately justified, teachers must be able to demonstrate progress made in this area through the use of detailed and appropriate recording systems. The regular collection and analysis of spontaneous communication samples such as those described in Chapter 1 would provide powerful supporting evidence for pupil development in this area (see Watson *et al.* (1989) for a useful spontaneous communication assessment).

Spontaneous communication samples recorded and analysed every four to six months, for example, would provide detailed evidence on progress in the following areas: how much children are communicating spontaneously; how they are communicating; the purpose of their communications; what they are communicating about.

Summary Points

- Practitioners in our study believed that the current curricular framework in England and Wales, with its emphasis on the teaching of the National Curriculum, does not sufficiently address the learning needs of children with autism and minimal or no speech.

- Practitioners said that the development of communication is a fundamental curricular aim for these children and therefore must form a curricular priority for them.

- Examples of rationales linked to research evidence are presented as guidelines for school-based documentation. Schools would need to develop their own specific guidelines.

Conclusions and Ways Forward

In this final chapter, a brief summary of project findings will be given. We emphasize the central role of a communication-enabling environment in developing a 'capacity' approach to working with individuals with autism and the crucial role played by staff training. We then consider some limitations of our present study and implications for future research.

The Study

This study analysed in detail the spontaneous communication of 18 young children with autism and minimal speech in the natural setting of their own schools. The early mental representational abilities of the children were also determined using a number of standardized assessments. The study examined both the attitudes and beliefs of staff and the influence of environmental factors in determining the quality of the communication-enabling environment.

Summary of Project Findings

1. Children with autism and minimal or no speech can and do communicate.

2. Teaching these children to communicate spontaneously for a number of purposes, and in a variety of everyday contexts, should be viewed as a major educational goal.

3. A range of social and environmental influences significantly affect the communication of these children.

4. Key social and environmental influences were identified as:

    - how adults talk and interact with children
    - the number and type of communication opportunities offered to children
    - how children are prompted to communicate
    - the effective teaching of systems of communication
    - effective classroom management
    - levels of motivation.

5. Environmental influences could have a disabling effect on the rate and quality of the children's communication.

6. The communication of these children can be significantly, and sometimes immediately, enhanced through the skilful use of an integrated range of strategies and approaches.

7. Teachers in our study believed that the current educational framework, with its emphasis on a subject-based National Curriculum, does not sufficiently address the learning needs of children with autism and minimal or no speech.

The Right to a Communication-Enabling Environment

All children have the right to live in a world where they can communicate their most basic needs and wants. From a therapeutic perspective, this would entail the establishment of a predictable communication-enabling environment, adaptable to the child's level of social and cognitive understanding, which provided a developmentally appropriate means of social interaction as its foundation. Crucial to the formation and maintenance of this environment are the skills, knowledge and attitudes of the staff responsible. These professional practices are influenced by levels of training and shaped by the way that autism is professionally constructed.

A Capacity Approach

Underlying the creation of such an environment must be a concept of autism which focuses on children's strengths and abilities in the areas of communication and social development, rather than on their often described impairment in these areas. As discussed earlier, popularly held views of autism are often inaccurate and misleading and may be derived, in part, from negative images portrayed in the media, which often depict children with autism as individuals who do not want to communicate with others. To give two representative examples: the *Daily Mail* reported that autism 'disrupts social and communication skills and leaves children isolated and disturbed' (1 April 1997); while *The Guardian* claimed that 'affected children and adults cannot relate to others in a meaningful way' (30 November 1994). Similar generalizations can also appear in the academic literature. Schaffer (1996), referring to the 'case of infantile autism', stated that 'some children, it appears, are constitutionally incapable of forming an attachment at all' (p.134).

As we have demonstrated, from the literature and our own research, such images are erroneous. They can, however, fundamentally influence people's concepts of what autism is and affect their expectations of what individuals with autism may or may not be able to achieve. Professionals involved in our study talked about the mismatch between popularly held beliefs and their own experiences of children's capabilities. One teacher commented:

> I think the general public regard people with autism as enclosed and trapped within their own world – so I think I came in [to teaching] with that expectation… I expected them not to be able to communicate with me…and found out very quickly that it wasn't true.

Another teacher reflected:

> When you read about autism, it seems very black and white 'These children do not form relationships, these children do not interact, these children do not play' and I don't feel it's like that at all – I think that's very misleading.

Certainly, it has be to recognized that people with autism do experience very significant difficulties in the areas of communication and social development as a result of their impairment, but this is very different from subscribing to a view that such individuals do not want to communicate, and cannot have meaningful relationships with others. Children with autism and minimal speech can and do communicate and they can and do make meaningful relationships with others. These can be significantly enhanced when they have access to communication environments that are enabling. Advice on the creation of such environments has formed a central theme of this book.

We subscribe to the 'capacity' model described by Booth and Booth (1993) who argued that 'new opportunities for the future emerge by focusing on a person's capacity as revealed in the context of their life experience, rather than on their deficiencies' (p.377). We would modify this statement by asserting that the optimum communicative and social capacities of children such as those in our study are best revealed in the context of communication-enabling environments, which have been arranged to take full account of their strengths and needs.

However, a focus on children's strengths is not sufficient. We have shown in this research that factors in the child's environment can be enabling or disabling, and these are environments provided by adults with positive attitudes, experience and training. Professional practices and attitudes, both intentional and unintentional, are shaped in part by the prevailing orthodox view on the nature of autism itself and how this is conceptualized.

Whittaker (1980) suggested that children seen as having profound and complex learning difficulties 'have tended to be identified in terms of what they could not do' (p.259). Two decades later this situation, in relation to children with autism and minimal speech, remains largely unchanged. We will briefly examine why this might be so. The triad of impairments (Wing and Gould 1979) forms the basis for the prevailing diagnosis of autism and it is the foundation for the two major diagnostic systems of autism: DSM-IV (American Psychiatric Association 1994) and ICD-10 (WHO 1987).

But the triad, in seeking to diagnose how people with autism differ from others, inherently focuses on what they cannot do. It is a *deficit model* where the deficit is located within the individual (Whittaker 1996). Our current work, however, suggests that environmental factors, as well as a focus on the strengths of the child, warrant further detailed examination in future research.

Training

We have considered the role of the environment and its enabling or disabling influence on the rate and quality of the children's spontaneous communication. In doing so there is no implied criticism of any of the professionals involved in this study, many of whom had specific qualifications and expertise in the field of autism. All of them were deeply concerned for the children's welfare and all provided stimulating environments, which employed well-accepted procedures for working with children with autism.

Our research highlights the need for specific and extensive training for staff working in this field, some of which can be undertaken in the context of short and distance learning courses. We believe, however, that the real requisite is extended full-time, specialist courses which involve assessment of competencies *in practice situations*, as well as the opportunities to relate this practice, in depth, to theoretical and professional issues. Only in this way will staff have the opportunity to acquire the range and quality of skills, professional knowledge and attitudes needed. Unfortunately, such courses have not existed within the UK in this field for well over a decade. They would require a significant allocation of resources over a protracted period of time.

Limitations and Suggestions for Future Research

Our results showed that, with this group of children with autism, factors within the environment, rather than factors within the children, emerged as statistically significant in determining the rate and complexity of their spontaneous communication. Although 18 is a reasonable number of children for an initial study, given the depth of the investigation, these children were located in only five specialist classrooms. How far a similar pattern of results will be found in other children, located in other environments, remains to be explored. It is very important that further research with similar groups of children is undertaken. These studies should observe the children and their environments in detail, for similar extensive periods, using comparable instruments to those employed in the present research, in a wider range of classrooms.

The average age of the children in our study was 4.5 years and 77 per cent of them were under 5 years. It is well known that many children with autism develop speech late (Lord and Paul 1997) so that some of the children in this study might be expected to go on to use speech. A follow-up study of the group and their environments might identify factors which could have predictive value in this regard.

Our focus on young children in this initial research was deliberate, as it is well known that early intervention is important for the future development of children with autism. But many children grow older without being given access to a conventional communication system, and we would like to see similar studies, and interventions, carried out with older groups. We would have some personal reservations about professionals using Proximal Communication with adolescents (see Whittaker 1996), even given the safeguards we outlined in Chapter 4, but all of the other procedures we have described could be of value with older students and adults and should be carefully evaluated in future research.

A further limitation of the present study is that the data were cross-sectional in nature. That is, information on a particular child was collected over a period of seven to ten days, with each classroom being observed for around a month on average. An important test of the approaches outlined in this book would be to see what effect they have had over a more protracted period of time by undertaking a longitudinal study of a group of children. Do the approaches lead to improvements in the children's abilities compared both to their own baseline level of skills, and to those of a matched group of children who have not followed the same approaches? We have been under-taking a longitudinal intervention research in a new project: Communication Intervention Research in Autism – United Kingdom (CIRA-UK), in order to begin to answer these questions.

In this book we have focused almost entirely on the professional aspects of implementing a range of essentially non-verbal approaches to communication within a minimal speech context. There are, however, important theoretical considerations underlying this work, particularly concerning the nature of the children's understanding of language, linked to environmental factors such as the different effects of complex and minimal adult speech on their behaviour, which we hope to be able to explore more fully in this new project. The role of language in autism has also been the subject of recent research by other groups, after a period of 25 years of relative neglect.

Since the mid-1970s, the major thrust of theoretical research in the UK has been aimed at identifying a cognitive difficulty as the fundamental impairment in autism. This cognitive focus had its origins in both the extensive and novel work of Hermelin and O'Connor (1970), and in the influential research by Bartak, Rutter and Cox (1975,1977). However, recent genetic studies of the families of people with autism have suggested that the children with and without speech may constitute different groups (Bolton et al. 1994) and that language may be an important component in this difference. The children who took part in the early studies by Bartak and his colleagues have been followed into adulthood in a major new study by Howlin, Marwood and Rutter (2000). This follow-up research has tentatively suggested that in autism 'the language impairment is far more central to the disorder and might underlie many other areas of dysfunction' (p.572) and 'the central deficit in autism might be a broader linguistic one' (p.574).

Howlin et al. (2000) are careful to point out that the relationship of these linguistic impairments to specific cognitive, behavioural and social difficulties in autism is likely to be complex. However, it seems likely to us that in the near future researchers will be carefully re-evaluating the role of language impairment in autism, and that different issues may arise for different groups within the autistic spectrum. The enabling or disabling role of adult speech in the children's environment should be a factor which is actively considered in future studies. We hope that our research, reported in this book, along with the results of our longitudinal study, may have some contribution to make to this debate.

Communication Intervention Research in Autism – United Kingdom (CIRA-UK)

We have had the opportunity of undertaking a longitudinal study of the approaches outlined in this book, over a two-year period, with some of the children drawn from the present research. We are continuing this work under the project title CIRA-UK (CIRA is pronounced /kee-ra/). Follow-up data from this research is currently being collected and we hope to analyse and publish it over the next two years (www.cira-uk.com).

Home-based Research

We have suggested that controlled intervention research, along with qualitative studies, be undertaken with a wider age range of children and in more classrooms to supplement the work we are undertaking in the CIRA-UK project. In addition we would very much like to see the approach evaluated in the home.

All of the procedures that we describe in this book have clear parallels in the natural home setting and we think that they could be adopted by families in ways which will assist, rather than disrupt, family life. Two members of our advisory group are parents and they have shared their valuable perspectives with us throughout the study.

Conclusion

The approaches outlined in this book are not offered as any sort of panacea, but we do have clear evidence that they were enabling for the children with autism in our study with whom they were employed. We hope that the ideas presented will be of practical benefit both to practitioners working with these children in school contexts and to families at home.

Children with autism and minimal speech are one of the most communicatively disempowered groups in our society. Future research could usefully focus on their strengths and needs, examined within the context of the enabling or disabling effects of their environment. The issue of enabling them to communicate spontaneously is also a vital one. We believe that the achievement of this goal lies not only in developing the skills and abilities of the individual with autism, but also in the establishment of high quality enabling environments which facilitate the development of their communication.

Appendix

Research Methods

We used the following research methods during data collection:

1. *Shadowing.* Children were shadowed for one whole school day during which time all of their spontaneous communication was recorded, using a schedule based upon Watson *et al.* (1989). Field notes relating to aspects of the prevailing communication environment were also made.

2. *Videotaping children,* for 10 minutes per child, in a range of everyday school situations: a group drinks session; a group educational task; a 1:1 teaching task; a 1:1 interaction setting; during independent workbox activity (Schopler *et al.* 1995); and for a period of free activity.

3. *Interviews.* Teachers and speech therapists working with the children were interviewed.

4. *Assessment tools* were used as follows: the Childhood Autism Rating Scale (Schopler *et al.* 1988); Vineland Adaptive Behaviour Scales (Sparrow, Ballarand and Cicchetti 1984); the Dunst (1980) assessment of cognitive abilities; the receptive scale of Reynell (1977); British Picture Vocabulary Scale (Dunn *et al.* 1982); Lowe and Costello's (1976) Symbolic Play Test, with an additional Object Substitution scale. This comprehensive list of procedures was designed to allow us to examine the early mental representational

abilities of the children, and to collect comparable data to our earlier research with non-verbal children with learning difficulties (Whittaker 1980, 1982, 1983, 1984a, 1984b).

In the present study findings were not compared across settings or methods for any of these procedures until all data had been collected.

Ethical Approaches to Research with Children with Autism

Increasingly researchers are becoming aware of the need to empower children participating in research through serious consideration of their rights and needs at all stages of the process: from the gaining of informed consent through to the presentation of research findings to them (Beresford 1997; Ward 1996). The ethical issues related to such aspirations are acknowledged to be both complex and problematic (Mahon *et al.* 1996; Morrow and Richards 1996). Empowerment of children with severe learning impairments in the research process has been viewed as particularly challenging, due to their limited cognitive understanding and expressive difficulties (Beresford 1997; Minkes, Robinson and Weston 1994).

Little has been written in this area regarding approaches to empowering children with autism who have minimal or no speech during the research process. Two key ethical points were of particular importance. First, we were committed to the notion that involvement in the research should be both as *enjoyable* and *meaningful* as possible for participating children. Second, we were determined that children taking part in the research should benefit directly from their participation.

To ensure meaningful and enjoyable involvement for children, we used the following approaches:

1.   A period was timetabled for both observing and interacting with the children in familiar environments, enabling them to get to know us and vice versa – an approach recently recommended by Ward (1996). This was done after the collection of the shadowing and video data and prior to the cognitive and language assessments.

2. Key familiar adults were interviewed informally so that we could obtain a detailed knowledge of each child's likes and dislikes, and their current means of communicating about them, so that they were respected throughout.

3. When working with individual children, we employed a *child-led* model of interaction, Proximal Communication, so that the children were able to control both the nature and length of the sessions.

4. Cognitive assessments were undertaken in settings familiar to the children and with the co-operation of staff who knew them well. Rapport with the children was established using Proximal Communication. As predicted, the cognitive and play tests were motivating to the children and carried out first. Some children showed discomfort at the language assessments and these were discontinued if this occurred. Sessions were generally videotaped for later analysis. Where practicable, Proximal Communication was used to end formal assessment sessions.

To secure the maximum direct and immediate benefits for the children from their participation, written feedback was provided for classroom teams and parents. Each classroom team received a detailed report containing information on each child's communicative profile, as well as practical suggestions for further enhancing the children's communicative development. These suggestions were discussed in a collaborative way with members of staff in oral feedback sessions. Feedback was given to each team within an average of three months (range 2–4 months). In this way staff had the opportunity to implement changes quickly if they believed that they would benefit the children. Parents received feedback reports that emphasized those approaches used by classroom teams which were clearly supporting the communicative development of their children.

Data Analysis

Data were analysed in a number of ways:

1. Shadowing data were examined with reference to the Watson *et al.* (1989) spontaneous communication schedule and to Wetherby and Prizant's (1989) assessment of communicative intent pro forma.

2. Field notes and interview data were analysed using a grounded theory approach, where categories for analysis emerge from the data.

3. For the 'Assessment of the Communication Environment' (Rowland and Schweigert 1993) four 10-minute samples of relevant classroom videotape were randomly selected for each school. A second independent analysis gave satisfactory inter-rater reliability.

4. Statistical analysis of aspects of the data was undertaken using a personal computer version of the *Statistical Package for the Social Sciences (SPSS)*.

Some Technical Details

The focus of the present study was on young children with autism and minimal speech, so group inclusion parameters were defined tightly to maintain homogeneity. The 16 boys and 2 girls had a mean Chronological Age (CA) of 54 months (range 35–80 months; *SD* 10.33), and all attended autism specialist classes within five special schools in England.

Only children who had an independent diagnosis of autism, from professionals experienced in this field, were considered for inclusion. Secondary evaluations using the Childhood Autism Rating Scale (CARS) confirmed the original diagnosis (Schopler *et al.* 1988). Two independent CARS were performed for each child. Inter-rater reliability was acceptable with no significant difference between the mean scores from the two sets of results ($t = 0.35$ df 17, $p = 0.73$). These data indicated that the children in the sample were all severely autistic (mean CARS 48; range 39–55; *SD* 4.85), with the majority being in the 'aloof' category (Wing and Attwood 1987).

Adaptive behaviour is concerned with how an individual copes with living in society. The Vineland Adaptive Behaviour Scale (Sparrow *et al.* 1984) has been widely used in this field (see Carter *et al.* 1998). Class teachers acted as informants and the overall Vineland Adaptive Behavioural Composite (ABC) ranged from 37 to 52 with a mean of 45.56 (*SD* 3.91). Based upon their Vineland scores, linked to Grossman (1983), three children would be seen as having mild learning difficulties, one had severe learning difficulties and 14 would have moderate learning difficulties at the time of assessment.

References

Abery, B. and Zajac, R. (1996) 'Self-determination as a goal for early childhood and elementary education.' In D. J. Sands and M. Wehemeyer (eds) *Self-Determination Across the Life Span*. London: Paul Brookes.

Alvin, J. and Warwick, A. (1992) *Music Therapy and the Autistic Child*. Oxford: Oxford University Press.

Alwell, M., Hunt, P., Goetz, L. and Sailor, W. (1989) 'Teaching generalized communicative behaviors within interrupted behavior chain contexts.' *Journal of the Association for Persons with Severe Handicaps 14*, 2, 91–100.

American Psychiatric Association (1994) *Diagnostic and Statistical Manual of Mental Disorders*, 4th edn. (DSM-IV). Washington DC: APA.

Ayres, B. J., Meyer, L. H., Erevelles, N. and Park-Lee, S. (1994) 'Easy for you to say: teacher perspectives on implementing the most promising practice.' *Journal of the Association for Persons with Severe Handicaps 19*, 2, 84–93.

Bannerman, D. J., Sheldon, J. B., Sherman, J. A. and Harchik, A. E. (1990) 'Balancing the right to habilitation with the right to personal liberties: the rights of people with developmental disabilities to eat too many doughnuts or to take a nap.' *Journal of Applied Behavior Analysis 23*, 1, 79–89.

Baron-Cohen, S. (1989) 'Perceptual role taking and protodeclarative pointing.' *British Journal of Developmental Psychology 7*, 113–127.

Bartak, L., Rutter, M. and Cox, A. (1975) 'A comparative study of infantile autism and specific developmental receptive language disorders. I. The children.' *British Journal of Psychiatry 126*, 127–145.

Bartak, L., Rutter, M. and Cox, A. (1977) 'A comparative study of infantile autism and specific developmental receptive language disorders. III. Discriminant functional analysis.' *Journal of Autism and Childhood Schizophrenia 7*, 383–396.

Bates, E., Benigni, L., Bretherton, I., Camaioni, L. and Volterra, V. (1979) *The Emergence of Symbols: Cognition and Communication in Early Infancy*. New York: Academic Press.

Beresford, B. (1997) *Personal Accounts: Involving Disabled Children in Research*. York: Social Policy Research Unit.

Berkell, D. E. (1992) 'Instructional planning: goals and practice.' In D. E. Berkell (ed) *Autism: Identification, Education and Treatment*. London: LEA.

Bolton, P., Macdonald, H., Pickles, A., Rios, P., Goode, S., Crowson, M., Bailey, A. and Rutter, M. (1994) 'A case-controlled family history study of autism.' *Journal of Child Psychology and Psychiatry 35*, 877–900.

Booth, W. and Booth, T. (1993) 'Accentuate the positive: a personal profile of a parent with learning difficulties.' *Disability, Handicap and Society 8*, 4, 377–391.

Bradshaw, J. (1998) 'Assessing and intervening in the communication environment.' *British Journal of Learning Disabilities 26*, 62–66.

Brown, F. and Cohen, S. (1996) 'Self determination and young children.' *Journal of the Association for Persons with Severe Handicaps 21*, 1, 22–30.

Bruner, J. S. (1975) 'The ontogenesis of speech acts.' *Child Language 2*, 1–19.

Carpenter, B. and Ashdown, R. (1996) 'Enabling access.' In B. Carpenter, R. Ashdown and K. Bovair (eds) *Enabling Access: Effective Teaching and Learning for Pupils with Learning Disabilities*. London: David Fulton.

Carr, E. G. and Kolinsky, E. (1983) 'Acquisition of sign language by autistic children II: spontaneity and generalization effects.' *Journal of Applied Behavior Analysis 16*, 3, 297–314.

Carter, A. S., Volkmar, F. R., Sparrow, S. S., Wang, J., Lord, C., Dawson, G., Fombonne, E., Loveland, K., Mesibov, G. and Schopler, E. (1998) 'The Vineland Adaptive Behavior Scales: supplementary norms for individuals with autism.' *Journal of Autism and Developmental Disorders 28*, 4, 287–302.

Charlop, M. H. and Haymes, L. K. (1994) 'Speech and language acquisition and intervention: behavioral approaches.' In J. L. Matson (ed) *Autism in Children and Adults*. Pacific Grove: Brooks/Cole.

Charlop, M. H., Schreibman, L. and Garrison Thibodeau, M. (1985) 'Increasing spontaneous verbal responding in autistic children using a time delay procedure.' *Journal of Applied Behavior Analysis 18*, 2, 155–166.

Charlop, M. H. and Trasowech, J. (1991) 'Increasing autistic children's daily spontaneous speech.' *Journal of Applied Behavior Analysis 24*, 747–761.

Christie, P. and Newson, E. (1998) *Teaching Pointing*. Nottingham: Early Years Centre.

Christie, P., Newson, E., Newson, J. and Prevezer, W. (1992) 'An interactive approach to language and communication for non-speaking children.' In D. A. Lane and A. Miller (eds) *Child and Adolescent Therapy: A Handbook*. Buckingham: Open University Press.

Christie, P. and Wimpory, D. (1986) 'Recent research into the development of communicative competence and its implications for the teaching of autistic children.' *Communication 20*, 1, 4–7.

Convention on the Rights of the Child: adopted by The General Assembly of the United Nations on 20th November, 1989. London: HMSO.

Coupe O'Cane, J. and Smith, B. (1994) *Taking Control: Enabling People With Learning Difficulties*. London: David Fulton.

Cox, M. V. (1991) *The Child's Point of View*. London: Harvester Wheatsheaf.

Curcio, F. (1978) 'Sensorimotor functioning and communication in mute autistic children.' *Journal of Autism and Childhood Schizophrenia 8*, 3, 281–292.

Curcio, F. and Paccia, J. (1987) 'Conversations with autistic children.' *Journal of Autism and Developmental Disorders 17*, 1, 81–93.

Dawson, G. and Galpert, L. (1990) 'Mothers' use of imitative play for facilitating social responsiveness and toy play in young autistic children.' *Development and Psychopathology 2*, 151–162.

DfEE (1999) *The Review of the National Curriculum in England.* London: HMSO.

Dunn, L. M., Dunn L. M., Whetton, C. and Pintilie, D. (1982) *British Picture Vocabulary Scale.* Windsor: NFER-Nelson.

Dunst, C. J. (1980) *A Clinical and Educational Manual for Use with the Uzgiris and Hunt Scales of Infant Psychological Development.* Baltimore: University Park Press.

Dyer, K. (1989) 'The effects of preference on spontaneous verbal requests in individuals with autism.' *Journal of the Association for Persons with Severe Handicaps 14*, 3, 184–189.

Elbers, L. and Ton, J. (1985) 'Play pen monologues: the interplay of words and babbles in the first words period.' *Journal of Child Language 12*, 551–565.

Eilers, R. E., Oller, D. K., Levine, S., Basinger, D., Lynch, M. P. and Urbano, R. (1993) 'The role of prematurity and socioeconomic status in the onset of canonical babbling in infants.' *Infant Behavior and Development 16*, 297–315.

Foster, S. H. (1990) *The Communicative Competence of Young Children.* London: Longman.

Goetz, L., Schuler, A. L. and Sailor, W. (1981) 'Functional competence as a factor in communication instruction.' *Exceptional Education Quarterly 2*, 51–60.

Gothelf, C. R., Crimmins, D. B., Mercer, C. A. and Finocchiaro, P. A. (1994) 'Teaching choice-making skills to students who are deaf-blind.' *Teaching Exceptional Children*, Summer, 13–15.

Grewe, T. S., Danhauer, K. J. and Thornton, A. R. (1994) 'Clinical use of otoacoustic emissions in children with autism.' *International Journal of Pediatric Otorhinolaryngology 30*, 2, 123–132.

Grossman, H. J. (1983) *Manual on Terminology and Classification in Mental Retardation.* Special Publication no. 2. Washington DC: American Association of Mental Deficiency.

Halle, J. (1987) 'Teaching language in the natural environment: an analysis of spontaneity.' *Journal of the Association for Persons with Severe Handicaps 12*, 1, 28–37.

Halpin, D. and Lewis, A. (1996) 'The impact of the national curriculum on twelve special schools.' *European Journal of Special Needs Education 11*, 1, 95–105.

Happé, F. (1994) *Autism: An Introduction to Psychological Theory.* London: UCL Press.

Hartup, W. W. (1999) 'Peer experience and its developmental significance.' In M. Bennett (ed) *Developmental Psychology: Achievements and Prospects.* Philadelphia: Psychology Press.

Hermelin, B. and O'Connor, N. (1970) *Psychological Experiments with Autistic Children.* Oxford: Pergamon Press.

Hewett, D. and Nind, M. (eds) (1998) *Interaction in Action.* London: David Fulton.

Hobson, R. P. (1993) *Autism and the Development of the Mind.* Hove: LEA.

Houghton, J., Bronicki, G. J. B. and Guess, D. (1987) 'Opportunities to express preferences and make choices among students with severe disabilities in classroom settings.' *Journal of the Association for Persons with Severe Handicaps 12,* 1, 18–27.

Howlin, P. and Rutter, M. (1987) *Treatment of Autistic Children.* Chichester: Wiley.

Howlin, P., Marwood, L. and Rutter, M. (2000) 'Autism and developmental receptive language disorder: a follow-up comparison in early adult life II: social, behavioural and psychiatric outcomes.' *Journal of Child Psychology and Psychiatry 41,* 5, 561–578.

Hubbell, R. D. (1977) 'On facilitating spontaneous talking in young children.' *Journal of Speech and Hearing Disorders 42,* 216–231.

Hurley-Geffner, E. (1995) 'Friendships between children with and without disabilities.' In R. L. Koegel and L. Kern Koegel (eds) *Teaching Children with Autism: Strategies for Initiating Positive Interaction and Improving Learning Opportunities.* Baltimore: Paul Brookes.

Jones, H. A. and Warren, S. F. (1991) 'Enhancing engagement in early language teaching.' *Teaching Exceptional Children,* Summer, 48–50.

Jordan, R. and Powell, S. (1992) 'Stop the reforms, Calvin wants to get off.' *Disability, Handicap and Society 7,* 1, 85–88.

Jordan, R. and Powell, S. (1995) *Understanding and Educating Children with Autism.* Chichester: Wiley.

Jordan, R. and Powell, S. (1997) 'Translating theory into practice.' In S. Powell and R. Jordan (eds) *Autism and Learning: A Guide to Good Practice.* London: David Fulton.

Kaufman, B. (1976) *To Love is to be Happy With.* London: Souvenir Press.

Kaufman, B. (1994) *Son Rise: the Miracle Continues.* California: Kramer.

Kaufman, S. L. (1998) 'The Son Rise program at the Option Institute.' *Communication,* Spring.

Kaye, K. (1977) 'Towards the origin of dialogue.' In H. R. Schaffer (ed) *Studies in Mother–Infant Interaction.* London: Academic Press.

Kennedy, C. H. and Haring, T. G. (1993) 'Teaching choice making during social interactions to students with profound disabilities.' *Journal of Applied Behavior Analysis 26,* 1, 63–76.

Kelly, V. (1994) 'Beyond the rhetoric and the discourse.' In G. M. and A. V. Kelly (eds) *The National Curriculum and Early Learning: An Evaluation.* London: Paul Chapman.

Kimbrough Olley, D. and Eilers, R. (1988) 'The role of audition in infant babbling.' *Child Development 59*, 441–449.

Klin, A. (1991) 'Young autistic children's listening preferences in regard to speech: a possible characterization of the symptom of social withdrawal.' *Journal of Autism and Developmental Disorders 21*, 1, 29–42.

Klin, A. (1993) 'Auditory brainstem responses in autism: brainstem dysfunction or peripheral hearing loss?' *Journal of Autism and Developmental Disorders 23*, 10, 15–35.

Koegel, R. L. and Wilhelm, H. (1973) 'Selective responding to the components of multiple visual cues by autistic children.' *Journal of Experimental Child Psychology 15*, 442–453.

Konstantareas, M. M., Mandel, L. and Homatidis, S. (1988) 'The language patterns mothers and fathers employ with their autistic boys and girls.' *Applied Psycholinguistics 9*, 403–414.

Landry, S. H. and Loveland, K. A. (1988) 'Communication behaviors in autism and developmental language delay.' *Journal of Child Psychology and Psychiatry 29*, 5, 621–634.

Leekham, S. R., Hunnisett, E. and Moore, C. (1998) 'Targets and cues: gaze-following in children with autism.' *Journal of Child Psychology and Psychiatry 39*, 7, 951–962.

Leung, J. P. and Chan, O. T. (1993) 'Teaching spontaneous verbal requests to Chinese children with autism using time delay procedure.' *Hong Kong Psychological Society Bulletin 30/31*, 47–57.

Levy, J (1999) 'Teaching critical social skills: utilizing attitude, environment, joining and motivation in the Son-Rise program.' *Autism99 Internet Conference: www.autism99.org*

Lewy, A. L. and Dawson, G. (1992) 'Social stimulation and joint attention in young autistic children.' *Journal of Abnormal Child Psychology 20*, 6, 555–566.

Lloyd, C. (1997). 'Inclusive education for children with special educational needs.' In S. Wolfendale (ed) *Meeting Special Needs in the Early Years: Directions in Policy and Practice*. London: David Fulton.

Lord, C. (1985) 'Autism and comprehension of language.' In E. Schopler and G. B. Mesibov (eds) *Communication Problems in Autism*. New York: Plenum Press.

Lord, C. and Paul, R. (1997) 'Language and communication in autism.' In D. J. Cohen and F. R. Volkmar (eds) *Handbook of Autism and Pervasive Developmental Disorders*. New York: Wiley.

Lovaas, O. I. (1977) *The Autistic Child*. New York: Irvington.

Lowe, M. and Costello, A. J. (1976) *The Symbolic Play Test*. Windsor: NFER.

McGhee, G., Daly, T., Izeman, S. G., Mann, L. H. and Risely, T. R. (1991) 'Use of classroom materials to promote preschool engagement.' *Teaching Exceptional Children*, Summer, 44–47.

McHale, S., Simeonsson, S., Marcus, M. and Olley, J. (1980) 'The social and symbolic quality of autistic children's communication.' *Journal of Autism and Developmental Disorders 10*, 299–310.

Mahon, A. C., Glendinning, C., Clarke, K. and Craig, G. (1996) 'Researching children: methods and ethics.' *Children and Society 10*, 145–154.

Marchman, V. A., Miller, R. and Bates, E. A. (1991) 'Babble and first words in children.' *Applied Psycholinguistics 12*, 1–22.

Matson, J. L., Sevin, J. A., Box, M. L. and Francis, K. L. (1993) 'An evaluation of two methods for increasing self-initiated verbalization in autistic children.' *Journal of Applied Behavior Analysis 26*, 3, 389–398.

Minkes, J. C., Robinson, C. and Weston, C. (1994) 'Consulting the children: interviews with children using residential respite care services.' *Disability and Society 9*, 1, 47–57.

Morrow, V. and Richards, M. (1996) 'The ethics of social research with children: an overview.' *Children and Society 10*, 90–105.

Mundy, P. and Crowson, M. (1997) 'Joint attention and early social communication: implications for research on intervention with autism.' *Journal of Autism and Developmental Disorders 27*, 6, 653–676.

Mundy, P., Sigman, M., Ungerer, J. and Sherman, T. (1986) 'Defining the social deficits of autism: the contribution of non-verbal communication measures.' *Journal of Child Psychology and Psychiatry 27*, 5, 657–669.

Newson, E. and Newson, J. (1975) 'Intersubjectivity and the transmission of culture: on the origins of symbolic functioning.' *Bulletin of British Psychology 28*, 437–446.

Newton, J. S., Horner, R. H. and Lund, L. (1991) 'Honoring activity preferences in individualized plan development: a descriptive analysis.' *Journal of the Association For Persons with Severe Handicaps 16*, 4, 207–212.

Nind, M. and Hewett, D. (1994) *Access to Communication*. London: David Fulton.

Nordoff, P., Robbins, C. and Britten, B. (1985) *Therapy in Music for Handicapped Children*. London: Victor Gollancz.

Owens, R. E. and Rogerson, B. S. (1988) 'Adults at the pre-symbolic level.' In S. N. Calculator and J. L. Bedrosian (eds) *Communication Assessment and Intervention for Adults with Mental Retardation*. London: Taylor and Francis.

Parsons, M. B. and Reid, D. H. (1990) 'Assessing food preferences among persons with profound mental retardation: providing opportunities to make choices.' *Journal of Applied Behavior Analysis 23*, 2, 183–195.

Peck, C. A. (1985) 'Increasing social opportunities for social control by children with autism and severe handicaps: effects on student behavior and perceived classroom climate.' *Journal of the Association for Persons with Severe Handicaps 10*, 4, 183–193.

Peck, C. A. (1989) 'Assessing social communicative competence: evaluating environments.' *Seminars in Speech and Language 10*, 1, 1–15.

Pelligrini, A. D. and Smith, P. K. (1998) 'Physical activity play: the nature and function of a neglected aspect of play.' *Child Development 69*, 3, 577–598.

Peterson, S. L., Bondy, A. S., Vincent, Y. and Finnegan, C. S. (1995) 'Effects of altering communicative input for students with autism and no speech.' *Augmentative and Alternative Communication 11*, 93–100.

Porter, J., Miller, O. and Pease, L. (1997) *Curriculum Access for Deaf-Blind Children.* London: HMSO.

Potter, C. A. (1996) 'A case study on aspects of the peer social relationships of a child with autism in a mainstream primary school.' Unpublished MEd thesis. University of Birmingham.

Potter, C. A. (1997) 'Responders or communicators? Teaching children with autism and learning disabilities to communicate spontaneously.' *Communication,* Winter, 27–28.

Potter, C. A. and Richardson, H. R. (1999) 'Facilitating classroom assistants' professional reflection through video workshops.' *British Journal of Special Education 26*, 1, 34–36.

Potter, C. A. and Whittaker, C. A. (1997) 'Teaching the spontaneous use of semantic relations through multipointing to a child with autism and severe learning difficulties.' *Child Language, Teaching and Therapy 13*, 2, 177–193.

Potter, C. A. and Whittaker, C. A. (1999) 'A minimal speech approach with children with little or no speech.' *Autism99 Internet Conference: www.autism99.org*

Powers, L. E., Wilson, R., Matuszewski, J., Philips, A., Rein, C., Schumacher, D. and Gensert, J. (1996) 'Facilitating adolescent self-determination: what does it take?' In D. J. Sands and M. L. Wehemeyer (eds) *Self-Determination Across the Life Span: Independence and Choice for People with Disabilities.* Baltimore: Paul Brookes.

Prevezer, W. (1990) 'Strategies for tuning into autism.' *Therapy Weekly*, October, 4–5.

Prizant, B. M. (1996) 'Communication, language, social and emotional development.' *Journal of Autism and Developmental Disorders 26*, 2, 173–177.

Prizant, B. M. and Wetherby, A. M. (1985) 'Intentional communicative behavior of children with autism: theoretical and practical issues.' *Australian Journal of Human Communication Disorders 13*, 2, 21–59.

Quicke, J. (1999) *A Curriculum for Life.* Buckingham: Open University Press.

Quill, K. (1995) *Teaching Children with Autism: Strategies to Enhance Communication and Socialization.* New York: Delamar.

Rapin, I. and Dunn, M. (1997) 'Language disorders in children with autism.' *Seminars in Paediatric Neurology 4*, 2, 86–92.

Reynell, J. K. (1977) *Reynell Developmental Language Scales.* Windsor: NFER.

Ricks, D. M. and Wing, L. (1975) 'Language, communication and the use of symbols.' *Journal of Autism and Childhood Schizophrenia 5*, 3, 191–221.

Robson, B. (1989) *Pre-school Provision for Children with Special Needs.* London: Cassell.

Rogers, S. (1996) 'Early intervention in autism.' *Journal of Autism and Developmental Disorders 26*, 2, 243–246.

Rosenthal Rollins, P., Wambacq, I., Dowell, D., Mathews, L. and Britton Reese, P. (1998) 'An intervention technique for children with autistic spectrum disorder: joint attention routines.' *Journal of Communication Disorders 31*, 2, 181–193.

Rowland, C. (1990) 'Communication in the classroom for children with dual sensory impairments: studies of teacher and child behavior.' *Augmentative and Alternative Communication 6*, 262–274.

Rowland, C. and Schweigert, P. (1993) *Analyzing the Communicative Environment (ACE).* Tucson: Communication Skill Builders.

SCAA (1994) *An Introduction to the Revised National Curriculum.* London: SCAA.

SCAA (1995) *Planning the Curriculum at Key Stages 1 and 2.* London: SCAA.

SCAA (1996) *Planning the Curriculum for Pupils with Profound and Multiple Learning Disabilities.* London: SCAA.

Schaffer, H. R. (1996) *Social Development.* Oxford: Blackwell.

Schopler, E. (ed) (1995) *Parent Survival Manual: A Guide to Crisis Resolution in Autism.* New York: Plenum Press.

Schopler, E., Mesibov, G. B. and Hearsey, K. (1995) 'Structured teaching in the TEACCH system.' In E. Schopler and G. B. Mesibov (eds) *Learning and Cognition in Autism.* London: Plenum Press.

Schopler, E., Reichler, R. J. and Renner, B. R. (1988) *The Childhood Autism Rating Scale (CARS).* Los Angeles: Western Psychological Services.

Schuler, A. L., Prizant, B. M. and Wetherby, A. M. (1997) 'Enhancing language and communication development: prelinguistic approaches.' In D. J. Cohen and F. R. Volkmar (eds) *Handbook of Autism and Pervasive Developmental Disorders.* New York: Wiley.

Sherborne, V. (1990) *Developmental Movement for Children.* Cambridge: Cambridge University Press.

Sherratt, D. (1999) 'The importance of play in good autism practice.' *Good Autism Practice 2*, 23–31.

Sigafoos, J., Kerr, M., Roberts, D. and Couzens, D. (1994a) 'Increasing opportunities for requesting in classrooms serving children with developmental disabilities.' *Journal of Autism and Developmental Disorders 24*, 5, 631–645.

Sigafoos, J. and Littlewood, R. (1999) 'Communication intervention in the playground: a case study on teaching requesting to a young child with autism.' *International Journal of Disability 46*, 3, 421–429.

Sigafoos, J., Roberts, D., Kerr, M. and Couzens, D. (1994b) 'Opportunities for communication in classrooms serving children with developmental disabilities.' *Journal of Autism and Developmental Disorders 24*, 3, 259–279.

Sigafoos, J. and York, J. (1991) 'Using ecological inventories to promote functional communication.' In J. Reichle, J. York and J. Sigafoos (eds) *Implementing Augmentative and Alternative Communication: Strategies for Learners with SLD.* Baltimore: Paul Brookes.

Sigman, M., Mundy, P., Sherman, T. and Ungerer, J. (1986) 'Social interactions of autistic, mentally retarded and normal children and their caregivers.' *Journal of Child Psychology and Psychiatry 27,* 5, 647–656.

Sparrow, S. S., Balla, D. A. and Cicchetti, D. V. (1984) *Vineland Adaptive Behavior Scales.* Minnesota: American Guidance Service.

Stalker, K. and Harris, P. (1998) 'The exercise of choice by adults with intellectual disabilities: a literature review.' *Journal of Applied Research in Intellectual Disabilities: A Literature Review 11,* 1, 60–76.

Stone, W. L. and Caro-Martinez, L. M. (1990) 'Naturalistic observations of spontaneous communication in autistic children.' *Journal of Autism and Developmental Disorders 20,* 4, 437–453.

Stone, W. L., Ousley, O. Y., Yoder, P. J., Hogan, K. L. and Hepburn, S. L. (1997) 'Nonverbal communication in two- and three-year-old children with autism.' *Journal of Autism and Developmental Disorders 27,* 3, 677–696.

Svavarsdottir, S. (1992) 'Spontaneous communication of children with autism in structured classrooms.' Unpublished MEd thesis. University of North Carolina.

Toomey, J. and Adams, L. A. (1995) 'Naturalistic observations of children with autism: evidence for intersubjectivity.' *New Directions in Child Development 69,* 75–89.

Trevarthen, C., Aitken, K., Papoudi, D. and Robarts, J. (1998) *Children with Autism: Diagnosis and Interventions to Meet Their Needs.* London: Jessica Kingsley Publishers.

Uzgiris, I. C. and Hunt, J. McV. (1989) *Assessment in Infancy: Ordinal Scales of Psychological Development,* 2nd edn. Illinois: University of Illinois Press.

van der Gaag, A. (1988) *Communication Assessment Profile (CASP).* London: Speech Profiles.

van der Gaag, A. and Dormandy, K. (1993) *Communication and Adults with Learning Disabilities.* London: Whurr.

Wall, M. E. and Dattilio, J. (1995) 'Creating option-rich environments: facilitating self-determination.' *Journal of Special Education 29,* 3, 276–294.

Ward, L. (1996) *Seen and Heard: Involving Disabled Children and Young People in Research and Development Projects.* York: Joseph Rowntree Foundation.

Ware, J. (1994) 'Classroom organisation.' In J. Ware (ed) *Educating Children with Profound and Multiple Learning Difficulties.* London: David Fulton.

Ware, J. (1996) *Creating a Responsive Environment for Pupils with Profound and Multiple Learning Disabilities.* London: David Fulton.

Watson, L. R., Martin, J. and Schaffer, B. (1986) 'Form, content and function of the spontaneous communication of autistic students.' *Australian Journal of Human Communications 14*, 1, 91–103.

Watson, L., Lord, C., Schaffer, B. and Schopler, E. (1989) *Teaching Spontaneous Communication to Autistic and Developmentally Handicapped Children.* New York: Irvington.

Wehemeyer, M. (1996) 'Self-determination as an educational outcome: why is it important for children, youths and adults with disabilities?' In D. J. Sands and M. Wehemeyer (eds) *Self-Determination Across the Life-Span: Independence and Choice for People with Disabilities.* Baltimore: Paul Brookes.

Wetherby, A. M. (1986) 'Ontogeny of communicative functions in autism.' *Journal of Autism and Developmental Disorders 16*, 3, 295–316.

Wetherby, A. M., Cain, D. H., Yonclas, D. G. and Walker, V. G. (1988) 'Analysis of intentional communication of normal children from the prelinguistic to the multiword stage.' *Journal of Speech and Hearing Research 31*, 240–252.

Wetherby, A. M. and Prizant, B. M. (1989) 'The expression of communicative intent: assessment guidelines.' *Seminars in Speech and Language 10*, 1, 77–91.

Wetherby, A. M. and Prizant, B. M. (1992) 'Facilitating language and communication.' In D. Berkell (ed) *Autism: Identification, Education and Treatment.* London: LEA.

Whittaker, C.A. (1980) 'A note on developmental trends in the symbolic play of hospitalised profoundly retarded children.' *Journal of Child Psychology and Psychiatry 21*, 3, 253–261.

Whittaker, C. A. (1982) 'Relational play, and the emergence of mental representation, in hospitalised profoundly retarded children.' *American Academy of Child Psychiatry*, Washington DC, October.

Whittaker, C.A. (1983) 'Non relational manipulative activity in hospitalised profoundly retarded children: play or stereotype?' *American Academy of Child Psychiatry*, San Francisco, October.

Whittaker, C. A. (1984a) 'Cognitive development, and aspects of prelinguistic and manual communication, in severely and profoundly retarded children' (by proxy). *American Academy of Child Psychiatry*, Toronto, October.

Whittaker C. A. (1984b) 'Aspects of play and language in children with profound learning difficulties.' Unpublished MEd thesis. University of Newcastle upon Tyne.

Whittaker, C. A. (1996) *Spontaneous Proximal Communication in Children with Autism and Severe Learning Disabilities.* Therapeutic Interventions in Autism, National Autistic Society: Autism Research Unit, Sunderland University.

Whittaker, C. A. and Potter, C. A. (1999a) 'Inclusive schools need an inclusive national curriculum.' In J. Swain and S. French (eds) *Therapy and Learning Difficulties: Advocacy, Participation and Partnership.* London: Butterworth-Heinemann.

Whittaker, C. A. and Potter, C. A. (1999b) 'Communication enabling environments for children with autism and minimal or no speech.' *Autism99 Internet Conference: www.autism99.org*

Whittaker, C. A. and Reynolds, J. (2000) 'Hand-signalling in dyadic Proximal Communication: social strengths of children with autism who do not speak.' *Child Language, Teaching and Therapy 16*, 1, 43–57.

World Health Organisation (1990) *International Classification of Diseases*, 10th revision. Geneva: WHO.

Wilkinson, C. (1994) 'Teaching pupils with PMLD to exert control.' In J. Coupe O'Cane and B. Smith (eds) *Taking Control: Enabling People with Learning Difficulties*. London: David Fulton.

Williams, R. (1991) 'Choices, communication and control: a call for expanding them in the lives of people with severe disabilities.' In L. H. Meyer, C. A. Peck and L. Brown (eds) *Critical Issues in the Lives of People with Severe Disabilities*. Baltimore: Paul Brookes.

Wing, L. and Attwood, A. (1987) 'Syndromes of autism and atypical development.' In D. J. Cohen and A. M. Donnellan (eds) *Handbook of Autism and Pervasive Developmental Disorders*. New York: Wiley.

Wing, L. and Gould, J. (1979) 'Severe impairments of social interaction and associated abnormalities in children: epidemiology and classification.' *Journal of Autism and Developmental Disorders 9*, 1, 11–29.

Wood, D., Wood, H., Griffiths, A. and Howarth, I. (1986) *Teaching and Talking with Deaf Children*. Chichester: Wiley.

Zanolli, K., Daggett, J. and Adams, T. (1996) 'Teaching preschool autistic children to make spontaneous initiations to peers using priming.' *Journal of Autism and Developmental Disorders 26*, 4, 406–422.

Subject Index

Author Index